Story Str

A screenwriter's guide to the six essential movie plot points and where to find them in 25 favorite movies

Naomi Beaty

Contents

Why we're here

In my years of working with and teaching screenwriters, one thing I can *always* count on is being asked for more movie examples.

Because, while every story is unique and brings its own challenges, most writers I've met still find it helpful to look at what's come before for guidance and inspiration. Checking out how other writers have handled their story's challenges can help us understand how our own stories work, show us what might be missing, or spark new ideas we hadn't thought of before.

Learning screenwriting theory is great, but there's nothing like seeing the principles in action to really wrap your brain around how something works. Looking at movie examples is also an opportunity to see the variety of ways that the theory you've learned can manifest in the real world.

This seems particularly true when it comes to story structure, which happens to be one of my favorite topics. I fell in love with story structure while working with Blake Snyder on his second book, *Save the Cat! Goes To the Movies*, and in the years afterward when I taught the Save the Cat! Weekend Intensives and my own workshop, Idea to Outline.

But long before I knew any of those experiences would come my way, I spent years trying to understand story structure. When I was just starting out, it felt difficult to connect the theory I read about in screenwriting books with what I was actually seeing in the movies I watched. And trying to apply the ideas to my own stories was frustrating and seemed all but impossible.

So this book, much like my first – *The Screenplay Outline Workbook* – is the resource I wish I'd had all those years ago. *Story Structure Made Easy* is intended both as a quick reference you can turn to while working on your current project, as well as an independent study guide of sorts, which you can refer to as you analyze movies to develop your understanding of story structure.

Inside you'll find brief summaries and analysis of 25 movies released between 1988 and 2022. And the information is intentionally organized in two different ways:

- **First, grouped by movie.** In this section you can get a feel for the overall shape and the significant turning points of each movie example. For each entry you'll find a logline (a one-sentence description of the story) and the movie's six Major Plot Points. As you read through these summaries, you'll get a sense of the whole story and see how the Major Plot Points relate to each other to take the audience on this movie's journey.

- **Second, grouped by structural plot point.** In this section you can compare and contrast the same plot point across all 25 movies. In this side-by-side comparison, you'll get a strong sense of that particular Major Plot Point's function within the larger story structure. I hope that seeing 25 examples of a given Major Plot Point all together will also help you brainstorm how that plot point might play out in your own story.

The plot point descriptions are deliberately brief and to the point. When I was in my early days of studying structure, I found most examples more confusing than clarifying. I wanted summaries that specified which event or scene was the actual plot point and why. So I've aimed to be as precise as possible while still providing enough context to grasp what's happening in the story and how the plot point works.

By now you may be wondering… what exactly are Major Plot Points? In case this is all new to you, I've included an overview of screenplay structure before we get to the examples. But for now, know that the Major Plot Points are the big turning points of any story. Taken together, they create a map through the story. A high level view of the whole territory.

And while I want to provide great examples to discuss and study, this isn't meant to be a paint-by-numbers template book. The goal isn't to create a soulless checklist, or to force your story into a box that doesn't suit it.

As you read through the examples, you may even disagree with my analysis from time to time, and that's okay. My goal is to help you understand the purpose and function of each of the Major Plot Points, and of story structure overall. But most importantly, I want to get you thinking about how stories work so that you can develop your own ideas about how to design powerful, entertaining experiences for your audience.

A last note:

This book is full of movies that I like to use as teaching examples, and some of my favorites to watch. I tried my best to represent a variety of genres, and to lean toward more recent movies and movies that perhaps hadn't been written about in other screenwriting books. Before you write in to tell me how many great movies I passed over… yes, I know.

By necessity, I needed some parameters for the movies I would analyze in this book. So much has already been written about the great movies of the 70's and earlier, and there are iconic movies that have been studied extensively in screenwriting books and articles. So rather than re-treading well-worn ground, I would like to continue the conversation, expanding and adding new examples to the mix.

Get *even more* screenwriting in your day!

Join 3,100+ readers and get the Write + Co. weekly memo straight to your inbox. It's like a {free} screenwriting class each week.

And when you sign up at the link below, you'll receive book bonuses and additional in-depth story analysis right away, and then my very best tips, strategies, and resources in one weekly article.

Sign up at writeandco.com/story-structure.

A Quick Guide to 3-Act Structure & Major Plot Points

To structure a story well is to arrange the events in a way that will engage and entertain an audience, and ultimately create a satisfying emotional experience.

Although we may pull a story apart and discuss individual components, structure is greater than the sum of its parts. Good structure – and effective story – happens because of the way the components relate to each other, compound and inform each other.

And yet, most of the time structure is invisible to the audience. Good structure is elegant and doesn't call attention to itself. But when structure is absent or weak, it's felt in the story's overall effect (or lack thereof).

You may have heard some negative opinions of story structure, or of popular story structure paradigms, which are sometimes accused of producing formulaic, "by the numbers" stories. And when structure is approached as nothing more than a checklist, that kind of bland, cookie-cutter story is likely to result.

But anyone approaching story structure that way is missing the point of it. The real point of story structure isn't to act as a template or set of non-negotiable rules to follow. It's a way to orchestrate an experience for the audience.

In this book we'll talk about common patterns in stories, but in the examples I hope to show a variety of ways that even traditionally structured stories can play out.

I don't want you to paint by numbers. My hope is to help you write movies that affect an audience, maybe even profoundly.

And that doesn't happen by checking off boxes just because a screenwriting book said so. It's far more important to understand what effect you're trying to achieve at each point in the story, if you hope to capture the audience's interest, engage their emotions, and deliver a satisfying experience – the true point of structure, and of storytelling.

Overview of 3-act structure

Within the entertainment industry, movies are most often discussed in the context of three-act structure. But I've worked with many writers who find the topic of story structure overwhelming, so if that's you – don't worry, you're not alone.

In this section we'll cover all the basics you need to know, starting with this high-level overview:

ACT 1	ACT 2	ACT 3
25%	50%	25%

The image above is the timeline of your screenplay or movie. For the sake of simplicity, let's say your script is 100 pages. (Industry standard is generally anywhere in the 85-120 range.)

Act 1 is approximately the first quarter of your script (25 pages or so). Act 2 is approximately the middle 50% of your script (from page 26 – 75 or so). And Act 3 is approximately the last 25% of your script (pages 76 – 100 or so).

Note: These numbers are *approximate*. There is no page that anything *must* happen on. The story has to entertain and move the audience – that's most important. So consider these numbers as guidelines to aim for, not rules that must be adhered to.

Each of the three acts has a purpose, a function in the story, and when taken all together they create a satisfying experience for the audience.

Act 1 is set up. It gives us the context we need to understand the story that's about to unfold. It's often said that movies basically come down to, "Someone wants something badly and goes after it against strong opposition." Act 1, then, establishes who wants what and what they're up against.

Act 2 is escalation, where the main thrust of the story plays out. In Act 2 we see the "someone" taking action, going after the "something" they want badly, and running into all of the stuff that's standing in their way – the conflict and obstacles.

Act 3 is resolution. It shows us the protagonist's final push to get what they want, the climactic confrontation, and the outcome of the main conflict. Who wins, who loses. Who gets what they want, who doesn't. Or maybe, who gets something unexpected that suits them better.

The Major Plot Points

The six Major Plot Points we'll focus on in this book are significant because together they determine the overall shape of the story.

If we're getting technical, the six Major Plot Points are made up of four plot *points* and two additional sections of the plot that are useful to include in order to get a full big-picture view. But that's splitting hairs a bit; let's agree they're important points in the plot and get to the useful stuff.

What are plot points? How do they function? And how do you know which plot points are major or otherwise?

The plot is the sequence of events in your story in which we track a character's pursuit of a goal or objective. A plot point is an event that changes the character's orientation to that objective.

At each plot point, the character is either closer to or farther from the goal. In that way, plot points mark progress and move the story forward.

The Major Plot Points are plot points just the same, but they have more specific and specialized functions. And the Major Plot Points work together to create a spine or throughline for the entire story.

The six Major Plot Points we'll look at to determine the story's overall shape are:

- Inciting Incident
- Break into Act 2
- Midpoint
- Low Point
- Break into Act 3
- Climax

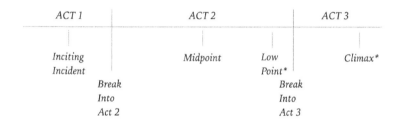

You may be used to calling these plot points by different names, and that's okay. What you call each one is less important than your understanding of the purpose and function.

Together, these plot points give you a high-level view of the entire story. They give us a feel for the whole shape of it even if we don't know every detail just yet.

And when you isolate and look at the Major Plot Points, what you see is that they relate to each other. They're not just a collection of arbitrary events. The Major Plot Points track the protagonist's progress in pursuit of the story goal.

Remember, that's what most movies boil down to: someone wants something badly and goes after it against strong opposition. The Major Plot Points are the most significant milestones or turning points in that journey. Together they create a spine that holds the story together.

Inciting Incident

The Inciting Incident usually occurs about 10-15 pages into the script (10-15 minutes into the movie), and you can think of it as the event that sets the story into motion or that shakes up the protagonist's normal world. (It's also known as the Catalyst, if you're a *Save the Cat!* fan.)

It is usually something that happens *to* the protagonist (as opposed to a choice or action *by* the protagonist). Often it's the first appearance or indication of the antagonist or main force of opposition.

The Inciting Incident very often fulfills its function (to kick the story into motion) by introducing a problem or opportunity that the protagonist must act on. That's how it sets things into motion: it creates circumstances in which the protagonist *must* take action, which soon leads to forming the story goal. (More on that in the next section.)

It's useful to note that the Inciting Incident doesn't have to be a negative event. Sometimes it looks more like an opportunity that the protagonist wants to take advantage of (rather than a problem to deal with), such as a job offer, a chance to compete for a big prize, or meeting a potential love interest.

And it's not unusual for an Inciting Incident to feel like both a problem *and* an opportunity, as you'll see in some of the example movies.

But whether the Inciting Incident feels like a problem or an opportunity (or both!), the effect we want it to achieve is the feeling of something happening, of that first domino falling. It's this story's plot events starting to move.

Break into Act 2

The Break into Act 2 is the turning point between Act 1 and Act 2, and you can think of it as the start of the Act 2 Adventure. (It's also known as Plot Point 1 if you're a Syd Field fan.)

Sometimes the Break into Act 2 is described as the event that locks the protagonist into the story. What that usually looks like is the protagonist acknowledging the main conflict, forming or declaring the story goal (the thing they're going to pursue in Act 2), or beginning to pursue the story goal in earnest.

By the time we get to this plot turn, which takes us from the setup (Act 1) into the meat of the story (Act 2), the audience is looking for a sense of where the movie is headed, what kind of story we're about to experience.

This plot point offers that sense of direction by solidifying the goal that the protagonist will pursue or the main conflict that we'll watch play out over the rest of the movie. That gives the audience something to track and helps us engage with your story, because it allows us to follow the progress toward the goal.

Midpoint

The function of the Midpoint is to create new tension. By this point in the movie, the main conflict needs more fuel on the fire to maintain the intensity – and the audience's interest – through the second half.

What happens at the Midpoint causes the audience to lean in with renewed interest or more emotional investment, or both. It makes us eager to stick around for the rest of the story.

To fulfill that function, a good Midpoint usually does one or both of these things in a big way: increase opposition, or raise the stakes. Think of it as anything that makes the story goal harder to achieve, or more important, urgent, or meaningful to achieve. Or all of the above.

A strong Midpoint can manifest in a variety of ways. Sometimes it looks like a big reveal, for the audience or the main character or both. Sometimes it's the start of a ticking clock. It can be a huge defeat or a huge win. It can be a "now it's personal" loss, or "sex at 60" moment (where a romantic relationship takes a major step).

After the Midpoint, good stories feel more intense, faster paced, more urgent, and higher stakes, and sometimes even drastically change their direction. And that effect is a direct result of what happens at the Midpoint.

Low Point

The Low Point is often described as the point where the protagonist seems furthest from reaching his or her goal. It can also look like the protagonist's worst nightmare coming to bear, or a huge new setback that the protagonist will have to overcome.

It might be where the protagonist loses their support system, such as if a mentor character dies, the love interest leaves, or the hero is fired from his position of responsibility or authority.

(If you're a follower of Save the Cat!, the Low Point we're talking about here includes the All is Lost and Dark Night of the Soul story beats.)

Putting the protagonist at a disadvantage creates tension as we fear a negative outcome, and that tension keeps us riveted as we prepare to move into the resolution phase of the story (Act 3).

And in stories where the protagonist wins in the end, taking us to rock bottom at the Low Point makes the eventual victory feel that much more earned and satisfying.

A good Low Point can also prime the audience for the final push toward the story goal by showing us how much it all means to the protagonist. What happens at the Low Point reinforces just how difficult this journey is and will continue to be, and it may be where the protagonist questions whether it's worth continuing on at all. If they decide that achieving the story goal is worth all the fight and struggle, we know how important it must be to them.

And the Low Point helps to show us the lasting emotional or psychological effect the experience is having on the protagonist. This is the place in the story where the character may first realize what they must learn or change going forward. We often see this thematic lesson reflected back to the protagonist here, even if they're not ready to accept it yet.

Break into Act 3

This plot point marks the start of the story's resolution. (It's also known as Plot Point 2, if you're a Syd Field fan.) Its function is to propel us into Act 3, to launch the line of action that will ultimately resolve the main conflict.

A hallmark of this plot point is the protagonist's new plan to achieve the story goal or new goal altogether. Sometimes it also showcases the protagonist's new, "growth" way of addressing the problem – now that he or she has been through the transformative events of this story.

The new plan, however nascent, far-fetched, or dangerous, will be the final attempt to achieve the story goal or resolve the main conflict. By stating or re-stating the story goal or plan to achieve it, the Break into Act 3 re-orients us, gets everyone on the same page, and gives us something to track as it launches us toward the big finish.

Climax

The Climax is the main character's final confrontation with the primary force of opposition. (It's also sometimes called the Final Battle, not to be confused with the *Save the Cat!* Finale beat.) The Climax ultimately shows us whether the protagonist achieves the story goal or not. It determines the outcome of the story's main conflict.

After the Climax, the audience will finally know whether the protagonist succeeds or fails, and then the movie is essentially over. We may need just a bit of wrap-up to bring a feeling of closure and satisfaction, but that's it. We're ready for the Fade Out.

One more thing to note about the Major Plot Points

As you read through the examples in this book, and as you identify the Major Plot Points in movies you watch, you'll start to recognize certain patterns for yourself. You'll notice common types of things that happen at an Inciting Incident, for example. And how those are likely different from a typical Climax.

You may also notice that some of the Major Plot Points tend to play out more quickly than others. Some land in the story with a sudden impact, creating a sharper turn. Others may occur over longer, more substantial scenes, or even short sequences of scenes.

How much weight, time, and space a Major Plot Point takes up affects rhythm and pacing, and contributes to the overall effect it creates in the story.

For example, the Inciting Incident is likely to happen in one scene. It's often a sudden, perhaps quick event. It can feel like a little explosion in the protagonist's normal day-to-day, or like a thunderbolt from the sky, as Michael Arndt (*Little Miss Sunshine*) has said. It can also be an event that puts the audience ahead of the protagonist, creating tension as we anticipate the moment when the character will become aware of and have to deal with this disruption.

The Break into Act 2 and Break into Act 3 are likely to feel like sharp or well-defined turns in the story, and to occur within one scene. (Even though there's plenty of context that's established leading up to these turning points.)

The Midpoint can feel like a sharp turn, especially if it spins the story in a drastically new direction. But it's just as likely to play out over a short series of scenes, a longer scene that's packed with important moments, or a big genre set piece.

The Low Point is less likely to happen in one moment or scene, and can span a series of scenes or even feel somewhat undefined, like a slow slide to rock bottom at the end of Act 2.

The Climax, too, will often play out over a sequence of scenes – which makes sense since it's the culmination of the whole story. Not only is there a lot to resolve and pay off, but the story's finale needs to feel significant, substantial, decisive.

There are no hard and fast rules, of course, about how any plot point must show up. Take this as an opportunity to see how the patterns create the recognizable movie rhythm we're familiar with, as well as which movies manage to do it differently to surprise, but still satisfy, the audience.

Examples, by movie

ABOUT A BOY (2002)

When a confirmed bachelor who eschews personal connections reluctantly befriends an awkward kid in need of a support system, the bachelor finds himself navigating real relationships for the first time and – if he can change his ways – maybe even love.

1. Inciting Incident: Lifelong bachelor Will is relieved when the single mom he's been dating breaks off their casual relationship. He has a sudden realization: dating single moms provides just what he needs – he can be "Will the good guy" for a short time before they inevitably move on for their own reasons, letting him off the hook before there's any expectation of going deeper or making a lasting commitment. This is the new opportunity that kicks the story into motion.

2. Break into Act 2: Will parts ways with awkward kid Marcus, who has unexpectedly entered Will's life through one of the single moms Will is trying to date. Marcus is going through a complicated time with his mom, Fiona, and Will wants no involvement. Here, Will drives away, fully intending to go back to his single, unattached life.

3. Midpoint: Fiona thinks the worst when she learns that Marcus and Will have been secretly spending time together. With Marcus in tow, she crashes Will's dinner at a fancy restaurant and demands an explanation. But by the end of the scene Fiona has decided that Marcus needs Will in his life. Marcus

invites Will to Christmas with his family, and Will can't say no.

Remembering that Will's story goal is to remain unattached, we can see how this plot point increases opposition (makes it harder to achieve that goal). It also raises the stakes, since now Will's relationship with Marcus is out in the open for others to see and judge.

4. Low Point: Will tries to come clean to Rachel, the girl he's recently met and fallen hard for, about a misunderstanding that's now spiraled into a big lie. But it's too little too late, she doesn't want to see him again, and he's heartbroken. A short time later Marcus asks Will for help, but Will is feeling too low and can't bring himself to step up. Marcus tells Will that Will doesn't care about anyone, and no one cares about Will.

5. Break into Act 3: Here, Will tries to go back to his old ways (recommitting to his original story goal), keeping himself busy with shallow pursuits and avoiding any deep or meaningful relationships. Will he succeed, or will he finally realize that "no man is an island"?

6. Climax: Will races to the school talent show to save Marcus from embarrassing himself and being ostracized by the other kids. But when he sees that Marcus is willing to do that in order to show Fiona how much he loves her, Will finally understands the thematic lesson this experience is meant to teach him, and does the same for Marcus. Will joins Marcus on stage, ultimately making himself the butt of the joke

so that Marcus can get through it unscathed. Rachel is in the audience and sees that Will might truly be a good guy after all. And in the end we see both Will and Marcus with genuine connections, surrounded by friends, family, and love.

BIG (1988)

When a 13-year-old boy makes a wish to be "big" and wakes in a grown man's body, he must navigate his new life as an adult until he can reverse the wish.

1. Inciting Incident: 13-year-old Josh wakes as a grown man. Mentally he's thirteen, physically he's 30. It's shocking and confusing and scary – and this is the new problem that kicks the story into motion.

2. Break into Act 2: Josh learns it will take six weeks to get a list of possible locations to find the Zoltar machine, which he needs in order to reverse the wish that made him "big." Until then he'll have to live on his own as an adult, which is what Act 2 is all about.

3. Midpoint: At a company party, co-worker Susan sets her sights on Josh, despite being romantically involved with another co-worker, Paul. Josh and Susan leave the party together. This raises the stakes as it marks the beginning of a new romantic relationship that will prove to be very meaningful for Josh. It also increases opposition since it makes Josh less likely to return to childhood as he builds an adult life he loves. And it also nicely ramps up the adversarial relationship with Paul for some added conflict in the story.

4. Low Point: By the end of Act 2, Josh's relationship with Susan is developing and he's actually becoming more and more the adult he looks like. He chooses spending time with Susan over childhood best friend

Billy, and Josh and Susan go on a date at a carnival where Josh is so focused on her, he doesn't even notice the Zoltar machine – the very thing that could reverse his "big" wish.

5. Break into Act 3: The list of possible Zoltar locations arrives in the mail at Billy's house. It's what Josh has been waiting for so he can reverse the wish, but Josh is so busy with work and Susan that he ignores Billy's call. It seems as though Josh has become fully entrenched in adulthood, and is content to stay there. The question we're now waiting on the answer to is: will Josh really choose to remain in adulthood, or will he realize the value and fleeting nature of childhood and go back to being thirteen?

6. Climax: Josh leaves what could be a career-making meeting and goes to find the Zoltar machine, where he makes a new wish to be a kid again. Susan finds him there and Josh must say goodbye to her before returning to his childhood home just as the magic wears off and he's restored to his 13-year-old self.

BLACK SWAN (2010)

After being cast as the lead in her ballet company's production of Swan Lake, an unstable young ballerina begins to unravel as she struggles to defend her role against a seductive and mysterious rival.

1. Inciting Incident: The ballet company's artistic director, Thomas, hand-selects dancers to audition for the role of Swan Queen, and Nina is among them. It's a demanding dual role made up of the innocent and fragile White Swan, Odette, and the sensual and dark Black Swan, Odile. Nina is desperate to win the role.

2. Break into Act 2: Nina learns she's been cast as Swan Queen. Always a bit of an outsider, the news immediately makes Nina the target of cattiness and jealousy from the other dancers.

3. Midpoint: Though she's pushing herself to her limit in rehearsals, Nina knows she continues to disappoint Thomas with her Black Swan performance. Then Nina learns that fellow ballerina Lily – whom Nina had cautiously believed to be a friendly ear – has revealed to Thomas things Nina said about him in confidence. Nina feels betrayed and, even worse, Thomas is angry. He tells Nina she could be brilliant but she's a coward, and to stop being so weak. Being on the verge of failure raises the stakes, and her sources of support disappearing increases opposition.

4. Low Point: Nina arrives late to dress rehearsal and finds Lily dancing in her place. Lily seems confused

when Nina mentions they spent the night before together, calling it Nina's fantasy. And then Nina's worst fear comes true when Lily is made her understudy. Nina spirals into despair, convinced that Lily is trying to sabotage and replace her.

5. Break into Act 3: Nina's solution is to practice even more. During which the pressure and stress bring on a psychotic break, with frightening hallucinations she now cannot escape.

6. Climax: Still hallucinating, Nina struggles to perform the opening night of Swan Lake. Between acts, Nina finds Lily in her dressing room. A confrontation turns into a fight and Nina kills her, hiding the body. Nina then takes the stage, dancing flawlessly as the Black Swan. Back in her dressing room she discovers Lily is still alive – and Nina realizes *she's* the one bleeding, having stabbed herself. But Nina goes on to dance the final act of the ballet, which ends with the White Swan throwing herself off a cliff. Nina wows the audience and the other dancers. She has achieved her story goal – to dance the role of Swan Queen. And as she lays dying on stage, Nina tells Thomas, "I felt it. It was perfect," as the screen fades to white.

BRIDESMAIDS (2011)

A down-on-her-luck young woman is asked to be her best friend's Maid of Honor, but finds herself struggling to defend both her position and her friendship when a rival bridesmaid makes it clear she has her sights set on taking over.

1. Inciting Incident: Annie's best friend, Lillian, announces her engagement and asks Annie to be her Maid of Honor. Annie's new problem is that she wants to hold onto her best friend, but Lillian is moving forward in life while Annie is stuck and unhappy – even though she won't admit it.

2. Break into Act 2: By the end of the engagement party, Annie has met rival Helen (as well as the other bridesmaids) and there's clearly tension there, but Lillian asks Annie to recommit and make the best of it. We can see the main conflict Annie is about to engage in; her story goal is to fend off Helen's attempts to show Annie up and take over as Maid of Honor and Lillian's best friend.

3. Midpoint: Annie accidentally ruins the bachelorette party, after which Lillian tells her Helen's going to be Maid of Honor from here on. Annie has lost her position in the wedding and, with their relationship now strained, is left struggling to hold onto her place as Lillian's best friend.

4. Low Point: At the bridal shower, Annie destroys any remaining goodwill with Lillian and is disinvited from the wedding altogether. It looks as though she's

ruined her friendship for good. On the way home Lillian also gets in a fight with good-guy love interest Officer Rhodes. She has failed at everything and is now at rock bottom.

5. Break into Act 3: We see Annie begin to change her ways, saying goodbye to her booty-call Ted. It's the start of her "growth" way of navigating the story. She may have lost everything, but she's also learned a (thematic) lesson and is finally ready to do things differently.

6. Climax: It's Lillian's wedding day but Annie learns she's nowhere to be found. Annie tracks Lillian down and gives her the pep talk (and dress re-design) Lillian needs in order to walk down the aisle. With this, Annie has repaired her friendship and is back in the wedding party.

CHILDREN OF MEN (2006)

In a dystopian near future in which the human race has become infertile, a disillusioned former activist agrees to help transport a miraculously pregnant woman across dangerous territory to a sanctuary at sea.

1. Inciting Incident: Theo, a disillusioned former activist, is grabbed off the street by kidnappers. The group turns out to include Theo's ex-wife, Julian, who up to now Theo has believed was dead. Now Julian asks Theo to use his connections to get a pair of exit visas, for a young woman Julian is trying to help.

2. Break into Act 2: Theo meets with the militant immigrant-rights group Julian is working with. Since Theo was only able to secure one of the exit visas they requested, they now want Theo to personally smuggle the young woman to Paris for them. He agrees but tells them after that, he's done.

3. Midpoint: Theo learns that members of their own group were responsible for killing Julian, so he escapes – taking with him the young woman, who we now know is miraculously pregnant. This plot point increases opposition since Theo has not only lost his support system, but he's also made enemies of them and they will hunt him down to recover the young woman.

4. Low Point: While Theo and the young woman are detained on a bus full of refugees, she goes into labor, which risks blowing their cover and puts them in

danger. They manage to hide her labor from the guards until they can make it off the bus to meet their contact. They're rushed to the stash house apartment just in time for the young woman to give birth.

5. Break into Act 3: The ally who was supposed to help Theo and the young woman get to safety has learned of the baby and now turns on them in an attempt to claim a reward. Theo fights him off and makes a quick getaway with the young woman and her baby. They're on their own again, still trying to reach their destination, now with a baby to protect.

6. Climax: As Theo and the young woman make their way through city streets that have erupted into a war zone, the militant group catches up to them, takes the girl and her baby captive, and orders that Theo be killed. Theo fights his way free, rescues the girl and baby, and manages to get them in sight of the boat to freedom. He dies before he sees them make it, but in his final moments he finally has hope for the future of humanity.

THE CONJURING (2013)

In the 1970's, a young family experiencing disturbing events at the secluded farmhouse they've just moved into calls on renowned paranormal investigators to document the occurrences and free the family from the mysterious terror.

1. Inciting Incident: The Perron family wakes their first morning at the secluded farmhouse they've just moved into, and everyone has complaints. One daughter smelled something rancid in the night, other daughters complain of the freezing temperatures in the house, and mom, Carolyn, has a strange new bruise. What's worse, the youngest daughter goes looking for the family dog – who refused to enter the house – and finds it dead outside. There's definitely something wrong with their new home.

2. Break into Act 2: During a game of hide-and-seek with youngest daughter April, Carolyn is lured in by a malevolent entity in the house. Although they don't know it yet, Carolyn is the true target of this haunting.

3. Midpoint: Married paranormal investigators Ed and Lorraine Warren tell the Perrons that the house needs an exorcism to rid them of the dark entity that's latched onto the family. But before the exorcism can be done, they must provide proof to the Catholic Church and get approval. So now the Warrens and Perrons must gather that evidence.

4. Low Point: Lorraine tells the others she knows what's going on: the evil entity "possesses the mother to kill

the child." This has been the pattern that's played out over and over again in and around this house for decades. Then the Perron daughters are attacked and thrown around the room – this can't go on or the family will be seriously injured, even killed. The Warrens want to go immediately to get approval from the church but before they leave, Lorraine is drawn to the lake by a child's voice. She has a vision of her own daughter, dead in the water. It's a warning.

5. Break into Act 3: The Perron family takes refuge at a motel, but Carolyn is acting very strange. Meanwhile, the Warrens meet with a priest and learn they'll need Vatican approval for the exorcism. They're told they'll have to wait and hope it comes in time, but we know the problem with Carolyn is going to force their hand – giving us the final showdown of Act 3.

6. Climax: Leading up to the climactic scene, the Warrens arrive at the house to find Carolyn trying to kill her daughter April. But when they try to remove Carolyn from the house, her skin begins to burn. Ed will have to perform the exorcism himself, in the house, with the others assisting – this story's final confrontation. During the exorcism, Lorraine helps Carolyn "fight from the inside," by prompting her to recall a happy family memory that Carolyn talked about earlier. Together the group fights off the entity until it's finally gone and Carolyn is free.

EDGE OF TOMORROW (2014)

In a future where humanity is losing a war with an alien race that can control time, a cowardly military public relations officer with no combat experience finds himself in an alien-created time loop, reliving the day of an enemy invasion over and over, until he can find a way to end the alien occupation.

1. Inciting Incident: Major William Cage, a cowardly military public relations officer with no combat experience, is demoted to Private and forced to join a squad of soldiers who will be the tip of the spear during the next day's dangerous mission.

2. Break into Act 2: Cage wakes up on a repeat of the day he originally arrived to join J Squad. The time loop is established and the Act 2 Adventure begins, wherein we'll watch Cage try to figure out what's happening to him (the time loop), why it's happening (so the aliens can win), and how to stop it (initially by convincing legendary soldier Rita to destroy the aliens and save the world, so he doesn't have to).

3. Midpoint: Frustrated and feeling resigned to his fate, Cage tries to run away from the fight on invasion day – something he hasn't done before. But by doing so he sees that the aliens will attack London next, and he knows he must return and find a way to save everyone. The threat of violence and danger extending beyond the battlefield raises the stakes and compels Cage to keep trying.

4. Low Point: Cage makes it to the location he's seen in his visions, where he believes he'll be able to destroy the alien, only to discover it's not there. He and Rita, the experienced soldier who's been helping him, try yet another strategy to locate the alien, but Cage is injured in the process and wakes in the hospital. He learns he's had a blood transfusion, which means he's lost the ability to reset time. If he dies now, he won't come back.

5. Break into Act 3: Cage and Rita make a new plan. They have three hours to kill the alien, and they need to recruit some soldiers who are crazy enough to follow them on this mission. Cage knows just the squad…

6. Climax: Rita and J Squad help Cage fight through an alien attack to reach the aliens' main location. With what looks like his last seconds alive, Cage manages to blow up the source, destroying the alien race's control of the world. When Cage wakes again, the world is different. Humans are victorious, and we know Cage was successful in achieving his story goal.

EVERYTHING EVERYWHERE ALL AT ONCE (2022)

A middle-aged laundromat owner learns she's the only person who may be able to save the multiverse from destruction by an evil entity, and she must jump between universes, tapping into the special skills of alternate versions of herself, in order to fight the threat.

1. Inciting Incident: Evelyn meets Alpha Waymond – an alternate-universe version of Evelyn's husband Waymond – when he cryptically warns Evelyn that she may be in grave danger, and gives her a strange set of instructions to follow.

2. Break into Act 2: Alpha Waymond gives Evelyn a choice: "Come with me and live up to your ultimate potential, or lie here and live with the consequences." She's reluctant but he carries her off... into the Act 2 Adventure.

   But the main conflict is truly locked in when, immediately afterward, we see that Jobu Tupaki – the one who threatens to destroy the multiverse – is a version of Evelyn and Waymond's own daughter Joy, and she is coming for Evelyn. Now we have all the context we need to understand what Evelyn is going to try to do (save the multiverse) and what she's up against.

3. Midpoint: While Alpha Waymond deals with Jobu Tupaki in another 'verse, in her own universe Evelyn tries to convince Waymond, Joy, and her father Gong

Gong what's happening. They laugh, not believing her. But then Gong Gong reveals to her that he is actually Alpha Gong Gong, and he directs Evelyn to kill Joy now so that Jobu has one less universe to access. Can Evelyn actually kill her own daughter in the hope of saving the multiverse? She refuses.

Now Evelyn doesn't want to just defeat Jobu, she specifically wants to save Joy – which increases the stakes. And this creates a new force of antagonism for Evelyn, as now Alpha Gong Gong and all the other Alpha jumpers are coming for her.

4. Low Point: The constant verse-jumping begins to take its toll on Evelyn and the life of each version of herself begins to suffer, finally culminating in Evelyn signing divorce papers just as her laundromat is seized by the IRS. Hopeless and seeing only the worst around her, Evelyn realizes she's become just like Jobu Tupaki.

5. Break into Act 3: Evelyn and Joy meet in another universe as other versions of themselves. Joy confesses that she had secretly hoped that she wouldn't be able to persuade Evelyn over to her nihilistic way of thinking. That perhaps Evelyn would see something she didn't and convince Joy all is not lost, there's another way. This is just enough to begin to turn Evelyn's thinking, giving her a new direction to pursue as she moves into Act 3.

6. Climax: Now fully embracing the thematic lesson, Evelyn finds "something to love" in each universe and uses kindness to battle and disarm each of her

opponents: the Alpha jumpers, Deirdre, Gong Gong, Jobu, and finally...

Evelyn and Joy face off in the real world as – despite everything – Joy asks Evelyn to just let her go. Evelyn refuses, telling Joy that no matter what else is possible or the other lives they might have had, and despite any pain involved, Evelyn chooses to be here with Joy and to cherish the few specks of time they have together. When they hug, we know Evelyn has fully accomplished her story goal.

EX MACHINA (2014)

A young programmer is recruited to an isolated estate to help his reclusive tech-genius employer test whether a new AI is truly sentient, but learns the tech genius has more nefarious intentions.

1. Inciting Incident: While at a luxurious but isolated estate, Caleb's reclusive tech genius employer, Nathan, tells Caleb about an amazing opportunity: Nathan has created an AI and wants Caleb to be the human component of a Turing test. This is an opportunity a guy like Caleb can't pass up – not only does he want to impress his employer, but it's also Caleb's chance to be part of a history-making event.

2. Break into Act 2: Discussing how to best test the AI he's created, Nathan and Caleb determine the real test goes beyond simulation. Is Ava (the AI) truly conscious? Nathan tells Caleb the question to investigate is how Ava feels about Caleb. We move into Act 2 with this direction in mind.

3. Midpoint: In this turning point scene, Caleb tells Ava about a thought experiment called "Mary in the black and white room." The story demonstrates the difference between a computer and the human mind. He explains: "The computer is Mary in the black and white room. The human is when she walks out," (and has experiences that cannot be taught or conveyed.) This is followed by a power outage, during which Ava tells Caleb she's responsible for the recent series of

outages that have occurred. She's causing them "so we can see how we behave when we are unobserved." Caleb is growing convinced that Ava possesses consciousness, and Ava now understands what she is missing out on – both of which raise the stakes in this story.

4. Low Point: Caleb learns that Nathan is planning a next model... and that means Ava will essentially be "killed" in the process. Then, Caleb sneaks a look at Nathan's files and sees videos of Nathan with earlier models – all eerily appear as women held captive. Nathan's girlfriend Kyoko then reveals to Caleb that she, too, is an android. Questioning reality, Caleb examines himself and cuts open his own arm to determine if he is an android as well.

5. Break into Act 3: Caleb tells Ava that she was right about Nathan and his nefarious intentions. Caleb has a plan for them to escape that night.

6. Climax: Caleb reveals to Nathan that he's modified the security system. They watch as Ava leaves her confinement and confers with Kyoko. Nathan knocks Caleb unconscious and rushes to stop them. He disables Kyoko and damages Ava in the process, but not before Nathan himself is stabbed. He lays dying while Ava repairs herself and then leaves Caleb locked inside the facility as she escapes on her own into the world.

GHOST (1990)

A murdered man's ghost recruits a reluctant psychic to help him keep his grieving girlfriend safe from the same men who killed him.

1. Inciting Incident: Walking home after a night out, Sam and Molly are mugged in an alley. Sam is shot and dies. But he's our hero, isn't he? Here, Sam's soul emerges from his body – he may be a ghost, but he remains the protagonist we'll follow through this story. Of course, being a ghost is a problem for Sam and we'll soon see why.

2. Break into Act 2: The man who shot Sam arrives at Molly's loft and Sam realizes his death wasn't part of a random mugging – and Molly is still in danger. Sam's story goal is now to keep Molly safe from the killer(s), which means first figuring out who this mugger-murderer is. And as a ghost, Sam is at a big disadvantage in trying to accomplish any of this.

3. Midpoint: Sam learns that his best friend, Carl, is connected to Willy Lopez – the mugger who killed Sam. Carl is the one who had Sam murdered, in an attempt to get the banking codes Sam carried in his wallet, which Carl needs in order to launder $4 million he's sitting on. Sam sees Carl instruct Willy to find and kill Oda Mae, the psychic who has been helping Sam.

   Each of these components raises the stakes, making Sam's pursuit of the story goal more personal, dangerous, and urgent. Carl is a friend and can easily get close to Molly, making her vulnerable to the danger. And since Carl has just ordered Oda Mae killed, we know the threat is real.

4. Low Point: While Sam is at Oda Mae's to warn her that she's in danger, Willy shows up to carry out Carl's orders to kill her. A chase ensues. Sam and Oda Mae narrowly escape.

Then, while Sam and Oda Mae are carrying out their own plan to move Carl's $4 million, Molly walks into the bank. Hearing that Oda Mae is using a different name, Molly becomes convinced Oda Mae is a con artist and the messages she conveyed from Sam were faked. This is an emotional low point for Sam, since he desperately wants to communicate with Molly and he's just lost any progress he'd made on that front.

5. Break into Act 3: Carl sees his money laundering account has been closed, and Sam "haunts" him by making "murderer" appear on the computer screen. This sends Carl back to Molly's to find out what's happening and where his money is... and Sam launches into the final push in pursuit of his story goal: keeping Molly safe.

6. Climax: Carl arrives at Molly's while Sam is in a weakened state. Molly and Oda Mae escape out the window and make it into the vacant loft above. They fight off Carl with Sam's help, and Carl is killed in the process. Molly is now safe; Sam's story goal is achieved. Afterward, we get a nice emotional payoff as well, when Molly is able to see Sam's ghost and he

finally tells her he loves her before the angels guide him away.

THE GREATEST SHOWMAN (2017)

The story of P.T. Barnum, as he rises from nothing to create an entertainment phenomenon, loses everything after becoming seduced by fame, and finds his way back to what truly matters – the friends and family who support him through it all.

1. Inciting Incident: P.T. receives the news that his employer is bankrupt and he's out of a job. This is a big problem, because although P.T. is ambitious and entrepreneurial-minded, he has no resources to fall back on and a family he's desperate to take care of.

2. Break into Act 2: P.T. has assembled a cast of "unique persons" and launches his new show! Something the world has never seen before – what we'll soon come to know as the circus. Signs go up, customers begin streaming in, and we enter Act 2 with the "Come Alive" musical set piece.

3. Midpoint: The Midpoint turn comes as P.T. introduces his new star, singer Jenny Lind, to the American high society audience. Stakes are raised because it's P.T.'s chance to finally get the respect he desires. We also see P.T. starting to lose sight of what really matters, as it's here that he tries to distance himself from his circus performers and keep them hidden away from his new, "respectable" crowd.

4. Low Point: P.T. has become so focused on touring with Jenny that he's letting down his circus performers, as well as his family. And now, Jenny lets

him know she wants more than a professional relationship. When P.T. declines, she feels used and says she'll leave the tour. This will ruin P.T., as he went into debt to secure the show venues. What's more, when P.T. returns home he finds the circus building burning to the ground. Everything is gone.

5. Break into Act 3: When P.T. learns his assistant, Carlisle, is in the burning building, P.T. runs in looking for him, risking his life to save his friend. P.T. has begun to embrace the thematic lesson, prioritizing the people that matter to him.

6. Climax: P.T. recommits himself to everyone who matters in his life. At the performers' insistence, he vows to find a way to restart the circus. He reunites with his wife, Charity. And he hands off ringmaster duties to Carlisle so P.T. can spend more time watching his daughters grow up. He's finally content with the life he's created.

HEAT (1995)

A career criminal and his loyal crew attempt to pull off a multi-million dollar bank robbery, while a dogged LAPD lieutenant and his team track them down.

1. Inciting Incident: LAPD's Robbery-Homicide team takes the case. What case? We've just seen a crew of criminals rob an armored truck and kill three guards in the process. That wasn't the original plan, but it happened, and now Neil – the leader of the crew – has to deal with his new problem: the "heat" is on their tail. Specifically, LAPD's Robbery-Homicide team, headed up by Lieutenant Hanna.

2. Break into Act 2: By the end of Act 1, Neil has set two jobs in motion, which together will be a payday his crew can retire on. The first involves selling the bearer bonds they've just stolen back to the owner, Van Zant. But unbeknownst to Neil, Van Zant has orders out to kill Neil's crew. The second job involves a $12 million bank heist. And they'll try to pull off both while Lt. Hanna and his Robbery-Homicide team actively chase down Neil and his crew. Those opposing forces create the main conflict we'll watch play out in Act 2.

3. Midpoint: Neil and his crew turn the tables. While under surveillance, they lure Hanna and his detectives out to show them Neil's onto them. This raises the stakes by taunting the detectives, and tipping them off also increases opposition. Not revealing he knew the

detectives were watching could have been an advantage, but Neil just couldn't resist.

4. Low Point: As Neil and his crew pull off their $12 million bank heist, Hanna's team intervenes and a huge shootout ensues. Neil's crew suffers injuries and losses. Afterward, Neil finds another of his crew at home, critically injured, and the man's wife has been murdered, too – done by Van Zant's men.

5. Break into Act 3: Neil calls his connection and asks for three things: Van Zant's address, information on the one-time crew member who has betrayed them, and a new "out" – a way to escape. We know what Neil now wants to accomplish by the end of the movie: revenge on both Van Zant and the traitor, and a clean getaway.

6. Climax: Neil is "home free" but he just can't leave when there's still an opportunity to get revenge on the former crew member who betrayed them. It's a fateful decision as doing so gives Hanna enough time to catch up to Neil, which brings us to the climactic chase scene. It's a cat-and-mouse game on the airport tarmacs, cop vs. robber. Mano a mano. Hanna finally manages to shoot Neil, who dies with Hanna looking on.

HIDDEN FIGURES (2016)

In 1960's Virginia, three Black female mathematicians pioneer vital roles at NASA as the United States races against Russia to be the first to put a man in space.

1. Inciting Incident: Katherine, a "computer" (a low-level mathematician at NASA), gets assigned to the Space Task Group. It's an exciting new position for her, but she's the first Black person to be allowed in this role, and there's a lot of pressure on her not to fail.

2. Break into Act 2: At the end of Katherine's first day in her new position, the director in charge of the Space Task Group, Al Harrison, speaks to her privately about the importance and difficulty of what they're doing. Sending a man into space, and ultimately to the moon, is completely unprecedented. They – and she – will have to "think differently" in order to succeed. Al tells her, "In my mind, I'm already there. Are you?" Katherine answers "yes"; she is on board and committed to the mission of the Space Task Group – and her Act 2 Adventure.

3. Midpoint: News breaks that the Russians have put the first man into space. Now, as Al Harrison says, the Americans are "second in a two-man race." So the stakes are raised and the Space Task Group – and Katherine, as part of it – has a new, more difficult goal: to get John Glenn into orbit and back safely.

4. Low point: Though Katherine also experiences some small personal wins along the way, several setbacks accumulate and compound by the time we reach the end of Act 2, creating a sense of tension and uncertainty about the outcome. The Liberty Bell capsule is lost, and Al Harrison has to go before Congress to convince them to let the STG continue their work at all. The IBM computer has arrived and is expected to make human "computers" obsolete. Paul Stafford – Katherine's immediate supervisor and nemesis – makes Katherine remove her name from reports, insisting that "computers" cannot author them, and her work is credited solely to Stafford. And time is ticking down to launch day but they still haven't figured out the math to get John Glenn safely back from orbit, so his life is at stake.

5. Break into Act 3: Collaborating with Al Harrison, Katherine has a math breakthrough that shows how they can get John Glenn home safely. This is the turn in the story that sends us toward the climax.

6. Climax: On the day of the launch, the IBM's calculations are off. Unless they can be sure of the landing coordinates they'll have to call off the launch and accept defeat. There's only one person John Glenn trusts to confirm the numbers: Katherine. When she's checked all the calculations and the launch is a go, Al Harrison brings her into the control room – recognizing her as a vital part of this mission. But before they can declare success, there's a tense moment as a warning light alerts the control room

that something has gone wrong. Working together, the team provides John Glenn with a manual override solution. Will Katherine's landing coordinates still work? Yes – John Glenn splashes down, safe. Everyone celebrates the accomplishment.

HUSTLE (2022)

A burnt-out NBA scout discovers a struggling young single father who is a talented street baller, and risks everything to make his own dream come true as he helps the player get a life-changing shot at going pro.

1. Inciting Incident: Stan, a burnt-out NBA scout, learns his mentor has passed away. This is a problem for Stan since his mentor just offered Stan the position he's been waiting for his whole life – on the team's coaching staff – but it hadn't been made official. For a moment his dream was within reach, but now Stan is back where he started and he's not happy about it.

2. Break into Act 2: Stan happens across talented Spanish street baller Boa Cruz. Stan realizes Boa could be the "missing piece" that new team owner Vin promised would be Stan's ticket back to a coaching position.

3. Midpoint: After a disappointing first scrimmage, Vin publicly declines to "pick up the tab" for Boa. Stan finally stands up to Vin and quits his job, opting to go all in on Boa. Stan now has six weeks to get Boa ready for and invited to the NBA scouting combine.

   This raises the stakes since Stan is betting his livelihood on Boa's success, now with nothing to fall back on. Boa's poor performance here makes that an even riskier proposition than before. And, what's more, we now have a real ticking clock – six weeks to make it all happen.

4. Low point: Stan has failed to get Boa an invitation to the combine. Even worse, Boa learns Stan has been lying to him about the team's interest. He tells Stan their partnership is over. Then we (and Boa) learn the story behind Stan's hand injury, when he "lost everything he wanted." He's been trying to redeem himself ever since. Later, Stan tries to call in one remaining favor to get Boa into the combine, to no avail. Stan feels like his entire life's work has been a waste, "it's like I wasn't even here."

5. Break into Act 3: The next morning, Stan's daughter gives him an idea to put Boa on social media and piggyback on family friend Dr. J's viral video fame. Stan is reluctant but his wife jumps in to help, making the phone call. This new strategy sends them into Act 3.

6. Climax: Stan's hard work and relationships prove to pay off as he and Boa get a chance to join a highly exclusive scouting showcase. With Stan's unwavering support, Boa feels the pressure lift and is able to deliver an impressive performance. Stan couldn't be more proud. Then Stan learns he's getting another chance to join the coaching staff, and all of his dreams have come true.

THE INVISIBLE MAN (2020)

After escaping her marriage to a brilliant but controlling inventor, a traumatized woman suspects her husband is using his "invisibility" technology to stalk and terrorize her, and she must convince friends, family, and the authorities to believe the truth before he kills her and everyone she loves.

1. Inciting Incident: Cecilia learns her estranged husband, Adrian, a brilliant but controlling inventor, has died by suicide. She's been in hiding since leaving their marriage and afraid of what he might do next, so this is an opportunity for Cecilia to finally be free of him.

2. Break into Act 2: Cecilia has been feeling a strange presence around her, but is unsure if it's real or if she's just paranoid. Here, she steps outside and what we see that she doesn't, is someone's breath behind her. There *is* someone stalking her, but he's invisible! This is the main conflict we'll be watching Cecilia deal with throughout Act 2.

3. Midpoint: Convinced Adrian is not actually dead, Cecilia discovers his cell phone and other personal items hidden in her attic, and then receives a text that reads, "Surprise." Cecilia craftily reveals Adrian's location by dumping a can of paint over him and a violent struggle ensues. Finally Cecilia manages to fight him off and escape the house. Now she's on the run from an invisible attacker, and he'll seemingly stop at nothing to get his revenge.

4. Low Point: Cecilia is in custody at a psychiatric hospital after being framed for killing her own sister. While there, she learns she's pregnant. Adrian's brother – Tom, an attorney who's handling Adrian's estate – visits Cecilia to tell her that she will no longer receive her $5 million inheritance (to the rest of the world Adrian is still dead) unless Cecilia agrees to return to Adrian and raise their child together. Now Cecilia knows Tom is in on it too, yet there's nothing she can do. Cecilia's only option may be to return to the husband she's been trying to escape all along.

5. Break into Act 3: Cecilia attempts suicide to lure out the invisible man and then stabs him, causing his suit to glitch temporarily. The facility's security team arrives but Adrian gets away. But before he does, he threatens to hurt those Cecilia loves, the last two people remaining in her support system. In Act 3, Cecilia must stop the invisible man.

6. Climax: Cecilia agrees to meet Adrian at his house to discuss mending their relationship, but secretly intends to get him to confess so she can record it as proof. When he won't admit all that he's done, she excuses herself. Moments later, the house security camera captures Adrian seemingly slitting his own throat. Cecilia discovers him and calls 911, appearing distraught. But once she's out of the camera's sight, she coolly watches as Adrian lies dying on the floor. When Cecilia leaves, we see she is carrying one of Adrian's "invisibility suits" in her purse, having orchestrated the whole thing.

JUMANJI: WELCOME TO THE JUNGLE (2017)

Four teenagers are magically transported into a jungle-themed video game and must work together to beat the game in order to escape.

1. Inciting Incident: While serving detention, four teenagers discover an old video game called "Jumanji," but when they try to play it they find themselves magically transported into the game.

2. Break into Act 2: The teens learn that a villain named Van Pelt has cursed the world of Jumanji, and they must return a jewel to its rightful place in order to lift the curse, save Jumanji, and escape the game. That gives us a clear roadmap of what they must do, and what we'll be watching for the rest of the movie.

3. Midpoint: The four teens discover the "missing piece" they've been tasked with finding in order to beat the level – and it turns out to be a fifth player who has been trapped in the game much longer and can help them navigate it. While this event gives them an advantage, it also raises the stakes by showing a potential future: being stuck in the game forever.

4. Low Point: The five players escape the game's bad guys in a helicopter, only to discover it's malfunctioning. By the skin of their teeth they manage to get it working on the fly and amidst a rhino stampede, but the jewel is lost in the process. The players have to backtrack into the herd of

dangerous rhinos in order to retrieve it. Just when they think they're in the clear, the fifth player is bitten by a mosquito – which, for his character, is a death sentence.

5. Break into Act 3: The players spot their final destination in the distance. Now all they have to do is find a way to get there and replace the jewel. But the villain knows where they are, and he's coming for them.

6. Climax: The villain closes in on the players but they work together and return the jewel to its home in spectacular video game hero fashion. The curse is lifted from Jumanji and the players return to their own world.

LITTLE MISS SUNSHINE (2006)

A dysfunctional, multi-generational collection of family members reluctantly embarks on a road trip together when the youngest of them gets a last-minute chance to fulfill her dream of competing in the Little Miss Sunshine pageant.

1. Inciting Incident: Olive, a young girl obsessed with beauty pageants, gets a phone call offering her a last-minute chance to compete in the Little Miss Sunshine contest, which is held several states away. In this ensemble movie, the phone call delivers an opportunity that Olive's whole family must deal with for one reason or another.

2. Break into Act 2: Once the whole family is (reluctantly) on board to make the road trip from Albuquerque to Redondo Beach so Olive can compete in the pageant, the story's setup is complete. The next morning they hit the road and we're off on the Act 2 Adventure.

3. Midpoint: The family stays overnight at a motel and the next morning Olive wakes her parents with alarming news: "Grandpa won't wake up." This plot event escalates things in a couple of ways. Notably, this unexpected medical emergency means their tight schedule is derailed and it becomes even less likely they'll make it to the pageant in time for Olive to compete. Also, since Grandpa is Olive's choreographer and coach, losing him means she's at a disadvantage going into the competition.

4. Low Point: The family races toward Redondo Beach under a nearly impossible deadline. But while on the road, Dwayne (Olive's teenage brother) learns he is colorblind – destroying his dream of becoming a fighter pilot. He demands to be let out of the car. With the family VW stopped on the side of the road and Dwayne refusing to continue on, it seems like the road trip may end here. This is especially gut wrenching since Dwayne's discovery is just the last in a series of disappointments for the members of this family.

5. Break into Act 3: Olive unselfishly shows Dwayne she's willing to let go of her own dream in order to support him, and that's enough to get him back in the car. The family gets back on the road for the final push to Olive's beauty pageant.

6. Climax: Olive takes the stage for her talent performance. Her family watches in the audience, terrified she'll be laughed off the stage. As Olive begins her routine the crowd soon realizes the moves Grandpa taught her are fit for a strip tease. Shocked by the "scandalous" show, the pageant organizer demands Olive be pulled off the stage. Instead, Olive's family joins her on stage to dance with wild abandon, having fun, regardless of what the rest of the world thinks.

THE POWER OF THE DOG (2021)

In 1920's Montana, a surly rancher sets out to destroy his brother's new wife with psychological torture, until the woman's medical student son arrives on summer break and an uneasy and sexually-charged relationship forms between the two men.

1. Inciting Incident: Peter and Phil cross paths for the first time when Phil and his ranch hands stop for dinner at Peter's mother's restaurant. Phil bullies and belittles the effeminate Peter, which is emotionally painful for both Peter and his mother, Rose. After dinner Phil's brother, George, overhears Rose crying in the kitchen and comforts her.

2. Break into Act 2: Phil warns George against marrying Rose, but George leaves to see her again, making his intentions clear. Phil immediately begins plotting against Rose's relationship with George.

3. Midpoint: Rose retrieves Peter from school so he can spend summer break with her at the ranch. Peter makes an offhand comment that lets us know he's dreading being around Phil. And Phil doesn't know it yet, but Peter's presence will have enormous consequences. For the audience, bringing Phil and Peter together in the same space again lights a fuse of tension that's riveting to watch burn down.

This plot point turns the action in a big way and increases the conflict since, as we'll come to find out,

Peter and Phil are more evenly matched than anyone yet realizes.

4. Low Point: Phil takes Peter under his wing. At first it's a way to further torture Rose, but soon Phil is surprised to learn he and Peter are more similar than he ever thought. Still, Phil's kindness can never really be trusted, so there's always a sense of unease around Phil and Peter's interactions, an impending doom we're dreading the arrival of. And while we probably don't realize the significance quite yet, it's here that we see Peter vow to Rose he'll fix her situation, and then Peter goes out alone to procure the tainted rawhide that will soon cause Phil's death.

5. Break into Act 3: Phil and Peter ride off together to work on a remote part of the ranch. Rose tries to protest, afraid of what might happen, but is unable to stop them. Only one of these men will prevail in the end.

6. Climax: Peter offers Phil some rawhide strips he's cut so that Phil can finish a lasso he's braiding. Phil is moved by this gesture and that night, Phil finishes braiding it as Peter looks on. The next morning, Phil has taken ill. Though he goes to the doctor, he dies quickly – likely from Anthrax. And now we realize the rawhide Peter supplied came from a diseased cow; he deliberately poisoned Phil in order to save Rose from the man's abusive behavior.

THE PROPOSAL (2009)

When a high-powered editor at a Manhattan publishing company learns she's about to be deported back to Canada, she convinces her long-suffering assistant to marry her for the Green Card, but first they must maintain their ruse at his family's weekend gathering as the couple prepares for their showdown with a suspicious immigration agent.

1. Inciting Incident: Margaret learns she's being deported and will lose her job. But she quickly lies and tells her employer that she and her assistant, Andrew, are engaged so she will soon have her green card. Now Margaret's problem is that reality doesn't match her lie, and she'll have to deal with it.

2. Break into Act 2: Struggling to appear as if they're really a couple, Margaret and Andrew arrive in Sitka, his hometown, for a weekend with his family. Cool city girl Margaret is clearly out of place as she meets Andrew's warm and down-to-earth mother and grandmother.

3. Midpoint: In a comedy of errors, Margaret and Andrew accidentally end up embracing, naked. This is the first time they've crossed that intimate line in any way. In the next scene, Margaret opens up to Andrew for the first time, and he tells her she's beautiful. Their attraction and feelings for each other are growing, which raises the stakes and complicates matters.

4. Low Point: Andrew's mom and grandmother surprise Margaret with a dress fitting, gifting her a wedding dress and jewelry that are meaningful family heirlooms. Margaret realizes she doesn't want to fool these kind, generous people. In addition to that, Margaret is really starting to care for Andrew and if she forces him to marry her in a sham wedding so she can stay in New York, she'll be responsible for taking him away from his family and standing between him and the possibility of real love.

5. Break into Act 3: Andrew's dad pulls Andrew and Margaret aside and calls their bluff. He's brought the suspicious immigration agent to Sitka and negotiated a deal for Andrew to go unpunished if he flips on Margaret. But Andrew sticks to their story and Margaret follows suit. The wedding is a go.

6. Climax: At the altar, Margaret confesses everything and takes responsibility for the ruse. She leaves with the immigration agent, ready to accept her punishment. Andrew goes after her, but is too late. Then, with his family's help, he races to the airport... but is too late again! Back in New York, Margaret is packing up her office when Andrew finally catches up with her and proposes – so they can start dating for real.

RATATOUILLE (2007)

A rat who dreams of being a chef gets the chance of a lifetime when he meets a kitchen grunt desperate to hold onto his job and the two secretly team up to bring a fading fine dining restaurant back to prominence, despite a head chef who wants them both gone.

1. Inciting Incident: Remy, a rat who dreams of being a chef, and his entire rat colony are forced to evacuate their home in the French countryside. In the process, Remy is separated from the other rats.

2. Break into Act 2: While observing the kitchen in the restaurant started by his recently deceased culinary idol, Chef Gusteau, Remy is horrified to see the restaurant's new garbage boy, Linguini, ruin that night's soup. Remy can't help but secretly jump in to fix it. He has impulsively started on his Act 2 Adventure, becoming a real chef.

3. Midpoint: Despite head chef Skinner's efforts to sabotage them, Remy and Linguini – who have since partnered in a Cyrano-esque kitchen ruse – improve on one of Gusteau's old recipes and become a hit with diners.
   This both increases opposition and raises stakes. It makes Skinner angry, and after this he'll redouble his efforts to expose the frauds. But the success with diners also puts Remy's dream that much closer and makes him want to be a real chef even more.

4. Low Point: Remy feels cast aside because Linguini has started following the lead of new girlfriend and fellow chef Colette. In retaliation, Remy breaks a promise to Linguini and allows the rat colony to raid the restaurant for food. In effect, Remy puts his chef dreams aside and reverts to the rat identity that's never felt quite right on him.

5. Break into Act 3: Adrift, Remy leaves both the restaurant and his rat family behind. He doesn't know where he belongs or where to go next, so at this point his "new plan" is simply to walk away from the things he now believes he's not meant for, or that aren't meant for him.

6. Climax: Remy seizes his dream and proves himself worthy when he commands chefs Linguini and Colette as well as the entire rat colony, to pull off a successful dinner service at the restaurant. Then, Remy finally reveals his true identity to famed food critic Anton Ego, who is convinced of Remy's talent and writes a glowing review – publicly hailing Remy as a chef.

SHAUN OF THE DEAD (2004)

When a 29-year-old slacker discovers a zombie outbreak has taken hold of his town, he must navigate now-dangerous terrain to get family, friends, and the ex-girlfriend he hopes to win back across town to safety before they're all turned into the living dead.

1. Inciting Incident: Outside a flower shop, protagonist Shaun sees a seemingly normal man savagely bite into a pigeon. What the heck is going on? There's something very wrong afoot, even if Shaun isn't exactly sure yet what it is. And he's a bit too preoccupied with his personal problems to really take notice, to be honest, but soon Shaun won't be able to ignore the new problem (zombies!).

2. Break into Act 2: Even though Shaun still isn't fully aware of the growing zombie infestation, *we* know that this is about to become his most urgent problem. Here, he wakes up after a night of drowning his sorrows to see a sign, literally, listing the To Do's he wrote for himself the night before: visit mom, win Liz back, "sort life out!" And we know we're watching Shaun try to accomplish the items on his list, while fighting off zombies. Now we're off on the Act 2 Adventure...

3. Midpoint: With his mom, stepdad, and best friend Ed in tow, Shaun arrives at Liz's. He runs inside to convince Liz to come with him to safety, and ends up with her friends David and Di as well. This scene

raises the stakes as Shaun has now taken on three more people, including the woman he wants to win back. He's responsible for everyone and there's a lot riding on their survival.

4. Low Point: Shaun discovers there's a zombie horde just outside the pub, trying to get in. What's worse, Shaun realizes, is that they followed *him* there. The place he convinced everyone to come to for safety has now been compromised, and by his own actions. Since Shaun's taken responsibility for keeping everyone alive, this is the ultimate failure.

5. Break into Act 3: Shaun discovers that the gun they'd assumed all this time was a prop gun, is real! Shaun now has a new plan to defeat the encroaching zombies, and we move into the final push in this fight for survival.

6. Climax: Remaining survivors Shaun, Liz, and Ed (who has been bitten but not yet fully turned) make it into the pub cellar where they're momentarily safe, but also trapped – with zombies beating down the door. Shaun laments that he failed everyone, and Liz tells him not to blame himself: "You did something, that's what counts." They quietly debate how to end it, as they only have two shotgun shells left between the three of them. But then Shaun gets one more idea – a possible escape plan. Ed won't go, knowing it's too late for him; he and Shaun must say their goodbyes here. With Ed distracting the zombies, Shaun and Liz make it outside, ready to keep fighting

for their lives… just as they see military forces arrive.
They didn't give up, and now they're saved!

THE SIXTH SENSE (1999)

After a fall from grace, a child psychologist gets a chance at redemption by helping a haunted young boy who has eerie similarities to an earlier client the doctor was tragically unable to save.

1. Inciting Incident: Malcolm, a child psychologist who is still traumatized from being shot by a former patient, reviews his notes as he waits to meet with a new child client, Cole. But Cole immediately scurries away instead of stopping to see Malcolm. Doing his job well is important to Malcolm, so a client who's reluctant to even speak with him is a problem Malcolm must find a way to solve.

2. Break into Act 2: When Cole tells Malcolm, "You can't help me," we know the main conflict is established and what we'll be watching Malcolm try to achieve over the course of the movie. Malcolm wants to help Cole, to treat him, but it will be a challenge since Cole won't willingly open up to him and doesn't believe there's anything Malcolm can do for him.

3. Midpoint: Malcolm confesses to Cole what happened with his former client, Vincent, who shot Malcolm and then himself. Reciprocating, Cole finally tells Malcolm his own secret: "I see dead people." But Malcolm can't believe this is true and fears the fact that Cole believes it means Malcolm hasn't helped him at all.

4. Low Point: By this point Malcolm is failing both professionally and personally. He not only fears he'll never be able to give Cole the help he needs, but because he's been so focused on Cole, Malcolm's marriage is suffering too. Something has to give. Malcolm tells Cole they can't work together anymore, but Cole begs Malcolm not to fail him. Then Cole learns Malcolm still doesn't believe him. Cole, feeling betrayed, asks, "How can you help me if you don't believe me?"

5. Break into Act 3: Looking for clues and some way forward, Malcolm goes back to the recordings of his old sessions with Vincent. And... he hears something. Malcolm is finally convinced Cole has been telling the truth, and Malcolm now has an idea about how to help him.

6. Climax: Malcolm goes with Cole to help one of the ghosts he's been seeing. It's a young girl who died after being poisoned by her own mother, and now wants to protect her sister from the same fate. This is the first time we've seen Cole unafraid of the ghosts, and able to use his gift to help them instead.

   A short time later, Malcolm watches Cole perform in his school play; Cole is now happy and surrounded by friends – Malcolm has finally succeeded at helping him.

SPIDER-MAN: INTO THE SPIDER-VERSE (2018)

After New York City teen Miles Morales is bitten by a radioactive spider and gains the powers of the superhero Spider-Man, he discovers he's just one of many other Spider-people across the multiverse, and they must all work together to disable villain Kingpin's Collider before it can destroy the city and everyone in it.

1. Inciting Incident: New York City teen Miles Morales is bitten by a radioactive spider. This creates both a problem and an opportunity for the protagonist: Miles is gaining superhero powers, but he's not sure that he wants them.

2. Break into Act 2: As the original Spider-Man lays dying, Miles makes a promise to him that he will finish Spider-man's mission and destroy Kingpin's Collider.

3. Midpoint: Miles and Peter B. Parker, an older, worn-down version of Spider-Man from another 'verse, work together to infiltrate Kingpin's research facility to steal the information they need in order to disable the Collider. While there, they are confronted by mad scientist Olivia Octavius, aka Doc Ock, who reveals that Peter will die from cellular decay if he remains in their dimension. An action set piece ensues as Doc Ock chases Peter and Miles through the lab and surrounding forest before Gwen Stacy, a

Spider-Woman from yet another dimension, ultimately rescues them.

4. Low Point: Miles is shocked to learn his beloved Uncle Aaron works for Kingpin and – after a fight between the Spider folk and Doc Ock and an assortment of baddies – Uncle Aaron learns Miles is a Spider-Man. Even though they're on opposing sides, Aaron can't bring himself to kill Miles, which prompts Kingpin to shoot Aaron. Shortly after, the collected Spider folk abandon Miles. They don't think Miles is ready to carry out their mission since he doesn't have full control of his Spider powers yet. Instead, Peter will be the one to see it through, even though this ensures Peter's death. On top of everything else, Miles won't get to avenge Aaron's death.

5. Break into Act 3: After a moving pep talk from his father, Miles is finally able to harness his Spider powers on command. He's ready, determined, and on the move... into Act 3, to complete his mission.

6. Climax: Miles and the rest of the Spider folk defeat Doc Ock and Kingpin's assortment of bad guys, and use the new override key they created to send the Spider folk home to their own dimensions. Then Miles alone faces off with Kingpin. Using his Spider powers and what he learned from his uncle, and buoyed by the love and support of his family, Miles throws Kingpin into the shutoff button. The Collider explodes and the city is saved.

TITANIC (1997)

A young socialite whose family and future depend on her upcoming marriage to a wealthy but controlling businessman falls for a struggling artist and must choose between the uncertainty of pursuing a life of passion, and the safety of the stifling existence planned for her – all while aboard the doomed maiden voyage of the Titanic.

1. Inciting Incident: Socialite Rose boards the Titanic for her return trip to America. At the same time, in a poker game, vagabond artist Jack wins tickets to board the Titanic too. His presence aboard the Titanic is what kicks Rose's story into motion.

   In stories where the main line of action is about a relationship, the Inciting Incident is very often when the two characters meet. Here, it's a little bit of a spin on the common pattern: fate is bringing the two of them together even if they don't know it yet.

2. Break into Act 2: Rose seeks out Jack to thank him for his help and discretion the night before, and they really begin to get to know each other in earnest. He seems to "get" her in a way her fiancé, Cal, doesn't, and Rose is fascinated by Jack's escapades and lifestyle of freedom. Their relationship begins.

3. Midpoint: It's a sequence that shows Rose choosing Jack and going all in. When Cal can't locate Rose, he sends his henchman, Lovejoy, to find her. Lovejoy learns Rose and Jack are together and chases them through the ship. They finally lose Lovejoy by hiding

in a car in the ship's cargo storage. Now alone, Rose says: "Put your hands on me, Jack." Meanwhile, Cal finds a note Rose left for him along with Jack's drawing of her in the nude. Rose knows what she wants now and she's not hiding it, but declaring it openly certainly increases opposition.

And then to really escalate the tension, the ship's lookouts spot an iceberg ahead!

4. Low Point: Jack tries to convince Rose to get on one of the few lifeboats that has room for her. Cal catches up to them and he concurs, promising that he's made an arrangement and can get himself and Jack on another lifeboat. Rose finally goes along, but once she's being lowered away Jack asks Cal, "There's no arrangement, is there?" Jack is doomed. It appears that the love of Rose's life is going to die and she won't be with him or even know for sure what's happened to him.

But at the last second Rose jumps out of the lifeboat, back onto the ship! She and Jack reunite – but Cal's seen it all and comes after them, armed with Lovejoy's gun.

5. Break into Act 3: Rose and Jack finally lose Cal, but they immediately run into flooding in the ship's lower corridors. At least they have each other, and they'll spend Act 3 trying to survive the disaster together.

6. Climax: Rose and Jack cling to wreckage in the freezing ocean water. Jack tells her, "Promise me you'll survive." Time passes and finally lifeboats come looking for survivors. Rose comes to and realizes it's

too late for Jack – he's already frozen to death. She musters the last of her strength and manages to alert the lifeboats that she is, indeed, alive.

Later, among the survivors, we see Rose avoid Cal. In case there was any question, she's not going back to that old life. At Ellis Island, she gives Jack's last name as her own.

TOP GUN: MAVERICK (2022)

An incomparable Naval aviator returns to the elite Top Gun flight school to train a new class of pilots, which includes the son of his former wingman, who died in a training exercise at the school decades earlier.

1. Inciting Incident: After Naval aviator "Maverick" angers a superior officer, hastening the end of Maverick's career, old friend Iceman, now an Admiral, intervenes on his behalf. Maverick is instead called back to Top Gun. It's an opportunity he desperately needs.

2. Break into Act 2: Class begins on the first day of training for their dangerous new mission. By now we know Maverick is there to teach younger pilots how to complete the mission, not fly it himself. The new class includes Rooster, the son of Maverick's late wingman, Goose, who died while flying with Maverick decades earlier. So we know what the main conflict is: Maverick's story goal is to teach these young pilots – Rooster in particular – how to fly the mission, and what he's up against includes the difficulty of the mission, Rooster's resentment toward him, and Maverick's own personal demons.

3. Midpoint: Maverick is summoned for a conversation with Iceman. In this scene, Maverick is in crisis. He doesn't want to have to send a young pilot off to fly a dangerous mission and potentially never return – especially if that pilot is Rooster, Goose's son. This

really drives home what's at stake for Maverick. And we finally understand why Maverick, a decorated fighter pilot, has never advanced in the ranks. He still carries the weight of Goose's death on his shoulders, and it affects the choices he makes. Iceman tells him, "The Navy needs Mav. The kid needs Mav. That's why you're still here." Despite being a "relic" and ruffling lots of feathers, Maverick hasn't outlived his usefulness yet, and this plot point nicely recommits Maverick to this mission – his last.

A scene that's lighter in tone but still important to the story follows Iceman's pep talk. We see Maverick and his class of young pilots playing dogfight football. He's one of them, and they're all one big team, bonding together. This helps to raise the stakes further since the more emotionally attached Maverick becomes, the harder it will be to send one of them off to possibly die, and the more it will hurt if he fails them.

4. Low Point: Maverick has been made team leader – he's going to fly the mission after all – and now he must announce which pilots will fly along with him. This is the thing he's been dreading. Ultimately, he chooses Rooster as his wingman, the last thing Maverick wants to do. But he knows he must show Rooster that he trusts and believes in him for the young man to succeed. So although it's killing Maverick, he makes the choice to send Rooster on the dangerous mission too.

5. Break into Act 3: Flightboss Cyclone orders, "Send them," and the four jets begin the mission. 'Will they all make it back?' is the question on our minds.

6. Climax: The pilots successfully complete their mission, but now they must get home – a dangerous endeavor in itself, and the part that matters most to Maverick. As they make their way through enemy territory, Rooster finds himself in danger and Maverick intervenes, saving him but getting shot down in the process. On the ground, Maverick is about to be shot but now Rooster intervenes, saving him and getting shot down himself. Which leads us into the final part of this story's climax, as we see Maverick and Rooster work together to get out of enemy territory and back to the aircraft carrier. Once Rooster is safely returned, Maverick's story goal is fully achieved.

Examples, by Major Plot Point

INCITING INCIDENT

- The event that sets the story into motion or that shakes up the protagonist's normal world.
- Usually something that happens *to* the protagonist (as opposed to a choice or action *by* the protagonist).
- Very often looks like the introduction of a problem or opportunity that the protagonist must act on. It sets the story into motion by prompting or forcing the protagonist to take action.
- Can be the first appearance or indication of the antagonist or main force of opposition, but it doesn't have to be a negative event. It can be an opportunity, like a job offer, a chance to compete for a big prize, or meeting a potential love interest.
- Often a sudden, perhaps quick event. Likely to happen in one scene.

About A Boy

Inciting Incident: Lifelong bachelor Will is relieved when the single mom he's been dating breaks off their casual relationship. He has a sudden realization: dating single moms provides just what he needs – he can be "Will the good guy" for a short time before they inevitably move on for their own reasons, letting him off the hook before there's any expectation of going deeper or making a lasting commitment. This is the new opportunity that kicks the story into motion.

Big

Inciting Incident: 13-year-old Josh wakes as a grown man. Mentally he's thirteen, physically he's 30. It's shocking and confusing and scary – and this is the new problem that kicks the story into motion.

Black Swan

Inciting Incident: The ballet company's artistic director, Thomas, hand-selects dancers to audition for the role of Swan Queen, and Nina is among them. It's a demanding dual role made up of the innocent and fragile White Swan, Odette, and the sensual and dark Black Swan, Odile. Nina is desperate to win the role.

Bridesmaids

Inciting Incident: Annie's best friend, Lillian, announces her engagement and asks Annie to be her Maid of Honor. Annie's new problem is that she wants to hold onto her best friend, but Lillian is moving forward in life while Annie is stuck and unhappy – even though she won't admit it.

Children of Men

Inciting Incident: Theo, a disillusioned former activist, is grabbed off the street by kidnappers. The group turns out to include Theo's ex-wife, Julian, who up to now Theo has believed was dead. Now Julian asks Theo to use his connections to get a pair of exit visas, for a young woman Julian is trying to help.

The Conjuring

Inciting Incident: The Perron family wakes their first morning at the secluded farmhouse they've just moved into, and everyone has complaints. One daughter smelled something rancid in the night, other daughters complain of the freezing temperatures in the house, and mom, Carolyn, has a strange new bruise. What's worse, the youngest daughter goes looking for the family dog – who refused to enter the house – and finds it dead outside. There's definitely something wrong with their new home.

Edge of Tomorrow

Inciting Incident: Major William Cage, a cowardly military public relations officer with no combat experience, is demoted to Private and forced to join a squad of soldiers who will be the tip of the spear during the next day's dangerous mission.

Everything Everywhere All At Once

Inciting Incident: Evelyn meets Alpha Waymond – an alternate-universe version of Evelyn's husband Waymond – when he cryptically warns Evelyn that she may be in grave danger, and gives her a strange set of instructions to follow.

Ex Machina

Inciting Incident: While at a luxurious but isolated estate, Caleb's reclusive tech genius employer, Nathan, tells Caleb about an amazing opportunity: Nathan has created an AI and wants Caleb to be the human component of a Turing test. This is an opportunity a guy like Caleb can't pass up – not only does he want to impress his employer, but it's also Caleb's chance to be part of a history-making event.

Ghost

Inciting Incident: Walking home after a night out, Sam and Molly are mugged in an alley. Sam is shot and dies. But he's our hero, isn't he? Here, Sam's soul emerges from his body – he may be a ghost, but he remains the protagonist we'll follow through this story. Of course, being a ghost is a problem for Sam and we'll soon see why.

The Greatest Showman

Inciting Incident: P.T. receives the news that his employer is bankrupt and he's out of a job. This is a big problem, because although P.T. is ambitious and entrepreneurial-minded, he has no resources to fall back on and a family he's desperate to take care of.

Heat

Inciting Incident: LAPD's Robbery-Homicide team takes the case. What case? We've just seen a crew of criminals rob an armored truck and kill three guards in the process. That wasn't the original plan, but it happened, and now Neil – the leader of the crew – has to deal with his new problem: the "heat" is on their tail. Specifically, LAPD's Robbery-Homicide team, headed up by Lieutenant Hanna.

Hidden Figures

Inciting Incident: Katherine, a "computer" (a low-level mathematician at NASA), gets assigned to the Space Task Group. It's an exciting new position for her, but she's the first Black person to be allowed in this role, and there's a lot of pressure on her not to fail.

Hustle

Inciting Incident: Stan, a burnt-out NBA scout, learns his mentor has passed away. This is a problem for Stan since his mentor just offered Stan the position he's been waiting for his whole life – on the team's coaching staff – but it hadn't been made official. For a moment his dream was within reach, but now Stan is back where he started and he's not happy about it.

The Invisible Man

Inciting Incident: Cecilia learns her estranged husband, Adrian, a brilliant but controlling inventor, has died by suicide. She's been in hiding since leaving their marriage and afraid of what he might do next, so this is an opportunity for Cecilia to finally be free of him.

Jumanji: Welcome to the Jungle

Inciting Incident: While serving detention, four teenagers discover an old video game called "Jumanji," but when they try to play it they find themselves magically transported into the game.

Little Miss Sunshine

Inciting Incident: Olive, a young girl obsessed with beauty pageants, gets a phone call offering her a last-minute chance to compete in the Little Miss Sunshine contest, which is held several states away. In this ensemble movie, the phone call delivers an opportunity that Olive's whole family must deal with for one reason or another.

The Power of the Dog

Inciting Incident: Peter and Phil cross paths for the first time when Phil and his ranch hands stop for dinner at Peter's mother's restaurant. Phil bullies and belittles the effeminate Peter, which is emotionally painful for both Peter and his mother, Rose. After dinner Phil's brother, George, overhears Rose crying in the kitchen and comforts her.

The Proposal

Inciting Incident: Margaret learns she's being deported and will lose her job. But she quickly lies and tells her employer that she and her assistant, Andrew, are engaged so she will soon have her green card. Now Margaret's problem is that reality doesn't match her lie, and she'll have to deal with it.

Ratatouille

Inciting Incident: Remy, a rat who dreams of being a chef, and his entire rat colony are forced to evacuate their home in the French countryside. In the process, Remy is separated from the other rats.

Shaun of the Dead

Inciting Incident: Outside a flower shop, protagonist Shaun sees a seemingly normal man savagely bite into a pigeon. What the heck is going on? There's something very wrong afoot, even if Shaun isn't exactly sure yet what it is. And he's a bit too preoccupied with his personal problems to really take notice, to be honest, but soon Shaun won't be able to ignore the new problem (zombies!).

The Sixth Sense

Inciting Incident: Malcolm, a child psychologist who is still traumatized from being shot by a former patient, reviews his notes as he waits to meet with a new child client, Cole. But Cole immediately scurries away instead of stopping to see Malcolm. Doing his job well is important to Malcolm, so a client who's reluctant to even speak with him is a problem Malcolm must find a way to solve.

Spider-man: Into the Spider-verse

Inciting Incident: New York City teen Miles Morales is bitten by a radioactive spider. This creates both a problem and an opportunity for the protagonist: Miles is gaining superhero powers, but he's not sure that he wants them.

Titanic

Inciting Incident: Socialite Rose boards the Titanic for her return trip to America. At the same time, in a poker game, vagabond artist Jack wins tickets to board the Titanic too. His presence aboard the Titanic is what kicks Rose's story into motion.

In stories where the main line of action is about a relationship, the Inciting Incident is very often when the two characters meet. Here, it's a little bit of a spin on the common pattern: fate is bringing the two of them together even if they don't know it yet.

Top Gun: Maverick

Inciting Incident: After Naval aviator "Maverick" angers a superior officer, hastening the end of Maverick's career, old friend Iceman, now an Admiral, intervenes on his behalf. Maverick is instead called back to Top Gun. It's an opportunity he desperately needs.

BREAK INTO ACT 2

- The turning point between Act 1 and Act 2. The start of the Act 2 Adventure.
- Usually looks like the protagonist acknowledging the main conflict, forming or declaring the story goal (the thing they're going to pursue in Act 2), or beginning to pursue the story goal in earnest.
- Creates a sense of direction and gives the audience something to track.
- Likely to feel like a sharp or well-defined turn in the story, and to occur within one scene.

About A Boy

Break into Act 2: Will parts ways with awkward kid Marcus, who has unexpectedly entered Will's life through one of the single moms Will is trying to date. Marcus is going through a complicated time with his mom, Fiona, and Will wants no involvement. Here, Will drives away, fully intending to go back to his single, unattached life.

Big

Break into Act 2: Josh learns it will take six weeks to get a list of possible locations to find the Zoltar machine, which he needs in order to reverse the wish that made him "big." Until then he'll have to live on his own as an adult, which is what Act 2 is all about.

Black Swan

Break into Act 2: Nina learns she's been cast as Swan Queen. Always a bit of an outsider, the news immediately makes Nina the target of cattiness and jealousy from the other dancers.

Bridesmaids

Break into Act 2: By the end of the engagement party, Annie has met rival Helen (as well as the other bridesmaids) and there's clearly tension there, but Lillian asks Annie to recommit and make the best of it. We can see the main conflict Annie is about to engage in; her story goal is to fend off Helen's attempts to show Annie up and take over as Maid of Honor and Lillian's best friend.

Children of Men

Break into Act 2: Theo meets with the militant immigrant-rights group Julian is working with. Since Theo was only able to secure one of the exit visas they requested, they now want Theo to personally smuggle the young woman to Paris for them. He agrees but tells them after that, he's done.

The Conjuring

Break into Act 2: During a game of hide-and-seek with youngest daughter April, Carolyn is lured in by a malevolent entity in the house. Although they don't know it yet, Carolyn is the true target of this haunting.

Edge of Tomorrow

Break into Act 2: Cage wakes up on a repeat of the day he originally arrived to join J Squad. The time loop is established and the Act 2 Adventure begins, wherein we'll watch Cage try to figure out what's happening to him (the time loop), why it's happening (so the aliens can win), and how to stop it (initially by convincing legendary soldier Rita to destroy the aliens and save the world, so he doesn't have to).

Everything Everywhere All At Once

Break into Act 2: Alpha Waymond gives Evelyn a choice: "Come with me and live up to your ultimate potential, or lie here and live with the consequences." She's reluctant but he carries her off... into the Act 2 Adventure.

But the main conflict is truly locked in when, immediately afterward, we see that Jobu Tupaki – the one who threatens to destroy the multiverse – is a version of Evelyn and

Waymond's own daughter Joy, and she is coming for Evelyn. Now we have all the context we need to understand what Evelyn is going to try to do (save the multiverse) and what she's up against.

Ex Machina

Break into Act 2: Discussing how to best test the AI he's created, Nathan and Caleb determine the real test goes beyond simulation. Is Ava (the AI) truly conscious? Nathan tells Caleb the question to investigate is how Ava feels about Caleb. We move into Act 2 with this direction in mind.

Ghost

Break into Act 2: The man who shot Sam arrives at Molly's loft and Sam realizes his death wasn't part of a random mugging – and Molly is still in danger. Sam's story goal is now to keep Molly safe from the killer(s), which means first figuring out who this mugger-murderer is. And as a ghost, Sam is at a big disadvantage in trying to accomplish any of this.

The Greatest Showman

Break into Act 2: P.T. has assembled a cast of "unique persons" and launches his new show! Something the world has never seen before – what we'll soon come to know as the circus. Signs go up, customers begin streaming in, and we enter Act 2 with the "Come Alive" musical set piece.

Heat

Break into Act 2: By the end of Act 1, Neil has set two jobs in motion, which together will be a payday his crew can retire on. The first involves selling the bearer bonds they've just stolen back to the owner, Van Zant. But unbeknownst to Neil, Van Zant has orders out to kill Neil's crew. The second job involves a $12 million bank heist. And they'll try to pull off both while Lt. Hanna and his Robbery-Homicide team actively chase down Neil and his crew. Those opposing forces create the main conflict we'll watch play out in Act 2.

Hidden Figures

Break into Act 2: At the end of Katherine's first day in her new position, the director in charge of the Space Task Group, Al Harrison, speaks to her privately about the importance and difficulty of what they're doing. Sending a man into space, and ultimately to the moon, is completely unprecedented. They – and she – will have to "think differently" in order to succeed. Al tells her, "In my mind, I'm already there. Are you?" Katherine answers "yes"; she is on board and committed to the mission of the Space Task Group – and her Act 2 Adventure.

Hustle

Break into Act 2: Stan happens across talented Spanish street baller Boa Cruz. Stan realizes Boa could be the "missing piece" that new team owner Vin promised would be Stan's ticket back to a coaching position.

The Invisible Man

Break into Act 2: Cecilia has been feeling a strange presence around her, but is unsure if it's real or if she's just paranoid. Here, she steps outside and what we see that she doesn't, is someone's breath behind her. There *is* someone stalking her, but he's invisible! This is the main conflict we'll be watching Cecilia deal with throughout Act 2.

Jumanji: Welcome to the Jungle

Break into Act 2: The teens learn that a villain named Van Pelt has cursed the world of Jumanji, and they must return a jewel to its rightful place in order to lift the curse, save Jumanji, and escape the game. That gives us a clear roadmap of what they must do, and what we'll be watching for the rest of the movie.

Little Miss Sunshine

Break into Act 2: Once the whole family is (reluctantly) on board to make the road trip from Albuquerque to Redondo Beach so Olive can compete in the pageant, the story's setup is complete. The next morning they hit the road and we're off on the Act 2 Adventure.

The Power of the Dog

Break into Act 2: Phil warns George against marrying Rose, but George leaves to see her again, making his intentions clear. Phil immediately begins plotting against Rose's relationship with George.

The Proposal

Break into Act 2: Struggling to appear as if they're really a couple, Margaret and Andrew arrive in Sitka, his hometown, for a weekend with his family. Cool city girl Margaret is clearly out of place as she meets Andrew's warm and down-to-earth mother and grandmother.

Ratatouille

Break into Act 2: While observing the kitchen in the restaurant started by his recently deceased culinary idol, Chef Gusteau, Remy is horrified to see the restaurant's new garbage boy, Linguini, ruin that night's soup. Remy can't help but secretly jump in to fix it. He has impulsively started on his Act 2 Adventure, becoming a real chef.

Shaun of the Dead

Break into Act 2: Even though Shaun still isn't fully aware of the growing zombie infestation, *we* know that this is about to become his most urgent problem. Here, he wakes up after a night of drowning his sorrows to see a sign, literally, listing the To Do's he wrote for himself the night before: visit mom, win Liz back, "sort life out!" And we know we're watching Shaun try to accomplish the items on his list, while fighting off zombies. Now we're off on the Act 2 Adventure...

The Sixth Sense

Break into Act 2: When Cole tells Malcolm, "You can't help me," we know the main conflict is established and what we'll be watching Malcolm try to achieve over the course of the movie. Malcolm wants to help Cole, to treat him, but it will be a challenge since Cole won't willingly open up to him and doesn't believe there's anything Malcolm can do for him.

Spider-Man: Into the Spider-Verse

Break into Act 2: As the original Spider-Man lays dying, Miles makes a promise to him that he will finish Spider-man's mission and destroy Kingpin's Collider.

Titanic

Break into Act 2: Rose seeks out Jack to thank him for his help and discretion the night before, and they really begin to get to know each other in earnest. He seems to "get" her in a way her fiancé, Cal, doesn't, and Rose is fascinated by Jack's escapades and lifestyle of freedom. Their relationship begins.

Top Gun: Maverick

Break into Act 2: Class begins on the first day of training for their dangerous new mission. By now we know Maverick is there to teach younger pilots how to complete the mission, not fly it himself. The new class includes Rooster, the son of Maverick's late wingman, Goose, who died while flying with Maverick decades earlier. So we know what the main conflict is: Maverick's story goal is to teach these young pilots – Rooster in particular – how to fly the mission, and what he's up against includes the difficulty of the mission, Rooster's resentment toward him, and Maverick's own personal demons.

MIDPOINT

- Creates new tension to sustain the main conflict through the second half of the movie.
- Usually does one or both of these things in a big way: increase opposition, or raise the stakes.
- After the Midpoint, good stories feel more intense, faster paced, more urgent, and higher stakes, and sometimes even drastically change their direction. And that effect is a direct result of what happens at the Midpoint.
- Can feel like a sharp turn, especially if it spins the story in a drastically new direction. But it's just as likely to play out over a short series of scenes, a longer scene that's packed with important moments, or a big genre set piece.

About A Boy

Midpoint: Fiona thinks the worst when she learns that Marcus and Will have been secretly spending time together. With Marcus in tow, she crashes Will's dinner at a fancy restaurant and demands an explanation. But by the end of the scene Fiona has decided that Marcus needs Will in his life.

Marcus invites Will to Christmas with his family, and Will can't say no.

Remembering that Will's story goal is to remain unattached, we can see how this plot point increases opposition (makes it harder to achieve that goal). It also raises the stakes, since now Will's relationship with Marcus is out in the open for others to see and judge.

Big

Midpoint: At a company party, co-worker Susan sets her sights on Josh, despite being romantically involved with another co-worker, Paul. Josh and Susan leave the party together. This raises the stakes as it marks the beginning of a new romantic relationship that will prove to be very meaningful for Josh. It also increases opposition since it makes Josh less likely to return to childhood as he builds an adult life he loves. And it also nicely ramps up the adversarial relationship with Paul for some added conflict in the story.

Black Swan

Midpoint: Though she's pushing herself to her limit in rehearsals, Nina knows she continues to disappoint Thomas with her Black Swan performance. Then Nina learns that fellow ballerina Lily – whom Nina had cautiously believed to be a friendly ear – has revealed to Thomas things Nina said about him in confidence. Nina feels betrayed and, even worse, Thomas is angry. He tells Nina she could be brilliant but she's a coward, and to stop being so weak. Being on the verge of failure raises the stakes, and her sources of support disappearing increases opposition.

Bridesmaids

Midpoint: Annie accidentally ruins the bachelorette party, after which Lillian tells her Helen's going to be Maid of Honor from here on. Annie has lost her position in the wedding and, with their relationship now strained, is left struggling to hold onto her place as Lillian's best friend.

Children of Men

Midpoint: Theo learns that members of their own group were responsible for killing Julian, so he escapes – taking with him the young woman, who we now know is miraculously pregnant. This plot point increases opposition since Theo has not only lost his support system, but he's also made enemies of them and they will hunt him down to recover the young woman.

The Conjuring

Midpoint: Married paranormal investigators Ed and Lorraine Warren tell the Perrons that the house needs an exorcism to rid them of the dark entity that's latched onto the family. But before the exorcism can be done, they must provide proof to the Catholic Church and get approval. So now the Warrens and Perrons must gather that evidence.

Edge of Tomorrow

Midpoint: Frustrated and feeling resigned to his fate, Cage tries to run away from the fight on invasion day – something he hasn't done before. But by doing so he sees that the aliens will attack London next, and he knows he must return and find a way to save everyone. The threat of violence and danger extending beyond the battlefield raises the stakes and compels Cage to keep trying.

Everything Everywhere All At Once

Midpoint: While Alpha Waymond deals with Jobu Tupaki in another 'verse, in her own universe Evelyn tries to convince Waymond, Joy, and her father Gong Gong what's happening. They laugh, not believing her. But then Gong Gong reveals to her that he is actually Alpha Gong Gong, and he directs Evelyn to kill Joy now so that Jobu has one less universe to access. Can Evelyn actually kill her own daughter in the hope of saving the multiverse? She refuses.

Now Evelyn doesn't want to just defeat Jobu, she specifically wants to save Joy –which increases the stakes. And this creates a new force of antagonism for Evelyn, as now Alpha Gong Gong and all the other Alpha jumpers are coming for her.

Ex Machina

Midpoint: In this turning point scene, Caleb tells Ava about a thought experiment called "Mary in the black and white room." The story demonstrates the difference between a computer and the human mind. He explains: "The computer is Mary in the black and white room. The human is when she walks out," (and has experiences that cannot be taught or conveyed.) This is followed by a power outage, during which Ava tells Caleb she's responsible for the recent series of outages that have occurred. She's causing them "so we can see how we behave when we are unobserved." Caleb is growing convinced that Ava possesses consciousness, and Ava now understands what she is missing out on – both of which raise the stakes in this story.

Ghost

Midpoint: Sam learns that his best friend, Carl, is connected to Willy Lopez – the mugger who killed Sam. Carl is the one who had Sam murdered, in an attempt to get the banking codes Sam carried in his wallet, which Carl needs in order to launder $4 million he's sitting on. Sam sees Carl instruct Willy to find and kill Oda Mae, the psychic who has been helping Sam.

Each of these components raises the stakes, making Sam's pursuit of the story goal more personal, dangerous, and urgent. Carl is a friend and can easily get close to Molly, making her vulnerable to the danger. And since Carl has just ordered Oda Mae killed, we know the threat is real.

The Greatest Showman

Midpoint: The Midpoint turn comes as P.T. introduces his new star, singer Jenny Lind, to the American high society audience. Stakes are raised because it's P.T.'s chance to finally get the respect he desires. We also see P.T. starting to lose sight of what really matters, as it's here that he tries to distance himself from his circus performers and keep them hidden away from his new, "respectable" crowd.

Heat

Midpoint: Neil and his crew turn the tables. While under surveillance, they lure Hanna and his detectives out to show them Neil's onto them. This raises the stakes by taunting the detectives, and tipping them off also increases opposition. Not revealing he knew the detectives were watching could have been an advantage, but Neil just couldn't resist.

Hidden Figures

Midpoint: News breaks that the Russians have put the first man into space. Now, as Al Harrison says, the Americans are "second in a two-man race." So the stakes are raised and the Space Task Group – and Katherine, as part of it – has a new, more difficult goal: to get John Glenn into orbit and back safely.

Hustle

Midpoint: After a disappointing first scrimmage, Vin publicly declines to "pick up the tab" for Boa. Stan finally stands up to Vin and quits his job, opting to go all in on Boa. Stan now has six weeks to get Boa ready for and invited to the NBA scouting combine.

This raises the stakes since Stan is betting his livelihood on Boa's success, now with nothing to fall back on. Boa's poor performance here makes that an even riskier proposition than before. And, what's more, we now have a real ticking clock – six weeks to make it all happen.

The Invisible Man

Midpoint: Convinced Adrian is not actually dead, Cecilia discovers his cell phone and other personal items hidden in her attic, and then receives a text that reads, "Surprise." Cecilia craftily reveals Adrian's location by dumping a can of paint over him and a violent struggle ensues. Finally Cecilia manages to fight him off and escape the house. Now she's on the run from an invisible attacker, and he'll seemingly stop at nothing to get his revenge.

Jumanji: Welcome to the Jungle

Midpoint: The four teens discover the "missing piece" they've been tasked with finding in order to beat the level – and it turns out to be a fifth player who has been trapped in the game much longer and can help them navigate it. While this event gives them an advantage, it also raises the stakes by showing a potential future: being stuck in the game forever.

Little Miss Sunshine

Midpoint: The family stays overnight at a motel and the next morning Olive wakes her parents with alarming news: "Grandpa won't wake up." This plot event escalates things in a couple of ways. Notably, this unexpected medical emergency means their tight schedule is derailed and it becomes even less likely they'll make it to the pageant in time for Olive to compete. Also, since Grandpa is Olive's choreographer and coach, losing him means she's at a disadvantage going into the competition.

The Power of the Dog

Midpoint: Rose retrieves Peter from school so he can spend summer break with her at the ranch. Peter makes an offhand comment that lets us know he's dreading being around Phil. And Phil doesn't know it yet, but Peter's presence will have enormous consequences. For the audience, bringing Phil and Peter together in the same space again lights a fuse of tension that's riveting to watch burn down.

This plot point turns the action in a big way and increases the conflict since, as we'll come to find out, Peter and Phil are more evenly matched than anyone yet realizes.

The Proposal

Midpoint: In a comedy of errors, Margaret and Andrew accidentally end up embracing, naked. This is the first time they've crossed that intimate line in any way. In the next scene, Margaret opens up to Andrew for the first time, and he tells her she's beautiful. Their attraction and feelings for each other are growing, which raises the stakes and complicates matters.

Ratatouille

Midpoint: Despite head chef Skinner's efforts to sabotage them, Remy and Linguini – who have since partnered in a Cyrano-esque kitchen ruse – improve on one of Gusteau's old recipes and become a hit with diners.

This both increases opposition and raises stakes. It makes Skinner angry, and after this he'll redouble his efforts to expose the frauds. But the success with diners also puts Remy's dream that much closer and makes him want to be a real chef even more.

Shaun of the Dead

Midpoint: With his mom, stepdad, and best friend Ed in tow, Shaun arrives at Liz's. He runs inside to convince Liz to come with him to safety, and ends up with her friends David and Di as well. This scene raises the stakes as Shaun has now taken on three more people, including the woman he wants to win back. He's responsible for everyone and there's a lot riding on their survival.

The Sixth Sense

Midpoint: Malcolm confesses to Cole what happened with his former client, Vincent, who shot Malcolm and then himself. Reciprocating, Cole finally tells Malcolm his own secret: "I see dead people." But Malcolm can't believe this is true and fears the fact that Cole believes it means Malcolm hasn't helped him at all.

Spider-Man: Into the Spider-Verse

Midpoint: Miles and Peter B. Parker, an older, worn-down version of Spider-Man from another 'verse, work together to infiltrate Kingpin's research facility to steal the information they need in order to disable the Collider. While there, they are confronted by mad scientist Olivia Octavius, aka Doc Ock, who reveals that Peter will die from cellular decay if he remains in their dimension. An action set piece ensues as Doc Ock chases Peter and Miles through the lab and surrounding forest before Gwen Stacy, a Spider-Woman from yet another dimension, ultimately rescues them.

Titanic

Midpoint: It's a sequence that shows Rose choosing Jack and going all in. When Cal can't locate Rose, he sends his henchman, Lovejoy, to find her. Lovejoy learns Rose and Jack are together and chases them through the ship. They finally lose Lovejoy by hiding in a car in the ship's cargo storage. Now alone, Rose says: "Put your hands on me, Jack." Meanwhile, Cal finds a note Rose left for him along with Jack's drawing of her in the nude. Rose knows what she wants now and she's not hiding it, but declaring it openly certainly increases opposition.

And then to really escalate the tension, the ship's lookouts spot an iceberg ahead!

Top Gun: Maverick

Midpoint: Maverick is summoned for a conversation with Iceman. In this scene, Maverick is in crisis. He doesn't want to have to send a young pilot off to fly a dangerous mission and potentially never return – especially if that pilot is Rooster, Goose's son. This really drives home what's at stake for Maverick. And we finally understand why Maverick, a decorated fighter pilot, has never advanced in the ranks. He still carries the weight of Goose's death on his shoulders, and it affects the choices he makes. Iceman tells him, "The Navy needs Mav. The kid needs Mav. That's why you're still here." Despite being a "relic" and ruffling lots of feathers, Maverick hasn't outlived his usefulness yet, and this plot point nicely recommits Maverick to this mission – his last.

A scene that's lighter in tone but still important to the story follows iceman's pep talk. We see Maverick and his class of young pilots playing dogfight football. He's one of them, and they're all one big team, bonding together. This helps to raise the stakes further since the more emotionally attached Maverick becomes, the harder it will be to send one of them off to possibly die, and the more it will hurt if he fails them.

LOW POINT

- Often described as the point where the protagonist seems furthest from reaching his or her goal. It can look like the protagonist's worst nightmare coming to bear, or a huge new setback that the protagonist will have to overcome.

- Putting the protagonist at a disadvantage creates tension to keep us riveted as we prepare to move into the resolution phase of the story.

- A rock bottom here makes an eventual victory feel that much more earned and satisfying.

- This is often where we see evidence of what this whole journey means to the protagonist, or how it's transforming their outlook, belief system, or approach to life.

- It's less likely to happen in one moment or scene, and can span a series of scenes or even feel somewhat undefined, like a slow slide to rock bottom at the end of Act 2.

About A Boy

Low Point: Will tries to come clean to Rachel, the girl he's recently met and fallen hard for, about a misunderstanding that's now spiraled into a big lie. But it's too little too late, she doesn't want to see him again, and he's heartbroken. A short time later Marcus asks Will for help, but Will is feeling too low and can't bring himself to step up. Marcus tells Will that Will doesn't care about anyone, and no one cares about Will.

Big

Low Point: By the end of Act 2, Josh's relationship with Susan is developing and he's actually becoming more and more the adult he looks like. He chooses spending time with Susan over childhood best friend Billy, and Josh and Susan go on a date at a carnival where Josh is so focused on her, he doesn't even notice the Zoltar machine – the very thing that could reverse his "big" wish.

Black Swan

Low Point: Nina arrives late to dress rehearsal and finds Lily dancing in her place. Lily seems confused when Nina mentions they spent the night before together, calling it Nina's fantasy. And then Nina's worst fear comes true when Lily is made her understudy. Nina spirals into despair, convinced that Lily is trying to sabotage and replace her.

Bridesmaids

Low Point: At the bridal shower, Annie destroys any remaining goodwill with Lillian and is disinvited from the wedding altogether. It looks as though she's ruined her friendship for good. On the way home Lillian also gets in a fight with good-guy love interest Officer Rhodes. She has failed at everything and is now at rock bottom.

Children of Men

Low Point: While Theo and the young woman are detained on a bus full of refugees, she goes into labor, which risks blowing their cover and puts them in danger. They manage to hide her labor from the guards until they can make it off the bus to meet their contact. They're rushed to the stash house apartment just in time for the young woman to give birth.

The Conjuring

Low Point: Lorraine tells the others she knows what's going on: the evil entity "possesses the mother to kill the child." This has been the pattern that's played out over and over again in and around this house for decades. Then the Perron daughters are attacked and thrown around the room – this can't go on or the family will be seriously injured, even killed. The Warrens want to go immediately to get approval from the church but before they leave, Lorraine is drawn to the lake by a child's voice. She has a vision of her own daughter, dead in the water. It's a warning.

Edge of Tomorrow

Low Point: Cage makes it to the location he's seen in his visions, where he believes he'll be able to destroy the alien, only to discover it's not there. He and Rita, the experienced soldier who's been helping him, try yet another strategy to locate the alien, but Cage is injured in the process and wakes in the hospital. He learns he's had a blood transfusion, which means he's lost the ability to reset time. If he dies now, he won't come back.

Everything Everywhere All At Once

Low Point: The constant verse-jumping begins to take its toll on Evelyn and the life of each version of herself begins to suffer, finally culminating in Evelyn signing divorce papers just as her laundromat is seized by the IRS. Hopeless and seeing only the worst around her, Evelyn realizes she's become just like Jobu Tupaki.

Ex Machina

Low Point: Caleb learns that Nathan is planning a next model... and that means Ava will essentially be "killed" in the process. Then, Caleb sneaks a look at Nathan's files and sees videos of Nathan with earlier models – all eerily appear as women held captive. Nathan's girlfriend Kyoko then reveals to Caleb that she, too, is an android. Questioning reality, Caleb examines himself and cuts open his own arm to determine if he is an android as well.

Ghost

Low Point: While Sam is at Oda Mae's to warn her that she's in danger, Willy shows up to carry out Carl's orders to kill her. A chase ensues. Sam and Oda Mae narrowly escape.

Then, while Sam and Oda Mae are carrying out their own plan to move Carl's $4 million, Molly walks into the bank. Hearing that Oda Mae is using a different name, Molly becomes convinced Oda Mae is a con artist and the messages she conveyed from Sam were faked. This is an emotional low point for Sam, since he desperately wants to communicate with Molly and he's just lost any progress he'd made on that front.

The Greatest Showman

Low Point: P.T. has become so focused on touring with Jenny that he's letting down his circus performers, as well as his family. And now, Jenny lets him know she wants more than a professional relationship. When P.T. declines, she feels used and says she'll leave the tour. This will ruin P.T., as he went into debt to secure the show venues. What's more, when P.T. returns home he finds the circus building burning to the ground. Everything is gone.

Heat

Low Point: As Neil and his crew pull off their $12 million bank heist, Hanna's team intervenes and a huge shootout ensues. Neil's crew suffers injuries and losses. Afterward, Neil finds another of his crew at home, critically injured, and the man's wife has been murdered, too – done by Van Zant's men.

Hidden Figures

Low point: Though Katherine also experiences some small personal wins along the way, several setbacks accumulate and compound by the time we reach the end of Act 2, creating a sense of tension and uncertainty about the outcome. The Liberty Bell capsule is lost, and Al Harrison has to go before Congress to convince them to let the STG continue their work at all. The IBM computer has arrived and is expected to make human "computers" obsolete. Paul Stafford – Katherine's immediate supervisor and nemesis – makes Katherine remove her name from reports, insisting that "computers" cannot author them, and her work is credited solely to Stafford. And time is ticking down to launch day but they still haven't figured out the math to get John Glenn safely back from orbit, so his life is at stake.

Hustle

Low point: Stan has failed to get Boa an invitation to the combine. Even worse, Boa learns Stan has been lying to him about the team's interest. He tells Stan their partnership is over. Then we (and Boa) learn the story behind Stan's hand injury, when he "lost everything he wanted." He's been trying to redeem himself ever since. Later, Stan tries to call in one remaining favor to get Boa into the combine, to no avail. Stan feels like his entire life's work has been a waste, "it's like I wasn't even here."

The Invisible Man

Low Point: Cecilia is in custody at a psychiatric hospital after being framed for killing her own sister. While there, she learns she's pregnant. Adrian's brother – Tom, an attorney who's handling Adrian's estate – visits Cecilia to tell her that she will no longer receive her $5 million inheritance (to the rest of the world Adrian is still dead) unless Cecilia agrees to return to Adrian and raise their child together. Now Cecilia knows Tom is in on it too, yet there's nothing she can do. Cecilia's only option may be to return to the husband she's been trying to escape all along.

Jumanji: Welcome to the Jungle

Low Point: The five players escape the game's bad guys in a helicopter, only to discover it's malfunctioning. By the skin of their teeth they manage to get it working on the fly and amidst a rhino stampede, but the jewel is lost in the process. The players have to backtrack into the herd of dangerous rhinos in order to retrieve it. Just when they think they're in the clear, the fifth player is bitten by a mosquito – which, for his character, is a death sentence.

Little Miss Sunshine

Low Point: The family races toward Redondo Beach under a nearly impossible deadline. But while on the road, Dwayne (Olive's teenage brother) learns he is colorblind – destroying his dream of becoming a fighter pilot. He demands to be let out of the car. With the family VW stopped on the side of the road and Dwayne refusing to continue on, it seems like the road trip may end here. This is especially gut wrenching since Dwayne's discovery is just the last in a series of disappointments for the members of this family.

The Power of the Dog

Low Point: Phil takes Peter under his wing. At first it's a way to further torture Rose, but soon Phil is surprised to learn he and Peter are more similar than he ever thought. Still, Phil's kindness can never really be trusted, so there's always a sense of unease around Phil and Peter's interactions, an impending doom we're dreading the arrival of. And while we probably don't realize the significance quite yet, it's here that we see Peter vow to Rose he'll fix her situation, and then Peter goes out alone to procure the tainted rawhide that will soon cause Phil's death.

The Proposal

Low Point: Andrew's mom and grandmother surprise Margaret with a dress fitting, gifting her a wedding dress and jewelry that are meaningful family heirlooms. Margaret realizes she doesn't want to fool these kind, generous people. In addition to that, Margaret is really starting to care for Andrew and if she forces him to marry her in a sham wedding so she can stay in New York, she'll be responsible for taking him away from his family and standing between him and the possibility of real love.

Ratatouille

Low Point: Remy feels cast aside because Linguini has started following the lead of new girlfriend and fellow chef Colette. In retaliation, Remy breaks a promise to Linguini and allows the rat colony to raid the restaurant for food. In effect, Remy puts his chef dreams aside and reverts to the rat identity that's never felt quite right on him.

Shaun of the Dead

Low Point: Shaun discovers there's a zombie horde just outside the pub, trying to get in. What's worse, Shaun realizes, is that they followed *him* there. The place he convinced everyone to come to for safety has now been compromised, and by his own actions. Since Shaun's taken responsibility for keeping everyone alive, this is the ultimate failure.

The Sixth Sense

Low Point: By this point Malcolm is failing both professionally and personally. He not only fears he'll never be able to give Cole the help he needs, but because he's been so focused on Cole, Malcolm's marriage is suffering too. Something has to give. Malcolm tells Cole they can't work together anymore, but Cole begs Malcolm not to fail him. Then Cole learns Malcolm still doesn't believe him. Cole, feeling betrayed, asks, "How can you help me if you don't believe me?"

Spider-Man: Into the Spider-Verse

Low Point: Miles is shocked to learn his beloved Uncle Aaron works for Kingpin and – after a fight between the Spider folk and Doc Ock and an assortment of baddies – Uncle Aaron learns Miles is a Spider-Man. Even though they're on opposing sides, Aaron can't bring himself to kill Miles, which prompts Kingpin to shoot Aaron. Shortly after, the collected Spider folk abandon Miles. They don't think Miles is ready to carry out their mission since he doesn't have full control of his Spider powers yet. Instead, Peter will be the one to see it through, even though this ensures Peter's death. On top of everything else, Miles won't get to avenge Aaron's death.

Titanic

Low Point: Jack tries to convince Rose to get on one of the few lifeboats that has room for her. Cal catches up to them and he concurs, promising that he's made an arrangement and can get himself and Jack on another lifeboat. Rose finally goes along, but once she's being lowered away Jack asks Cal, "There's no arrangement, is there?" Jack is doomed. It appears that the love of Rose's life is going to die and she won't be with him or even know for sure what's happened to him.

But at the last second Rose jumps out of the lifeboat, back onto the ship! She and Jack reunite – but Cal's seen it all and comes after them, armed with Lovejoy's gun.

Top Gun: Maverick

Low Point: Maverick has been made team leader – he's going to fly the mission after all – and now he must announce which pilots will fly along with him. This is the thing he's been dreading. Ultimately, he chooses Rooster as his wingman, the last thing Maverick wants to do. But he knows he must show Rooster that he trusts and believes in him for the young man to succeed. So although it's killing Maverick, he makes the choice to send Rooster on the dangerous mission too.

BREAK INTO ACT 3

- Marks the start of the story's resolution phase. Launches the line of action that will ultimately resolve the main conflict.
- Often where we see the protagonist recommit to their story goal, come up with a new plan to achieve the goal, or sometimes declare a new goal altogether.
- It orients us, gets everyone on the same page, and gives us something to track as it sends us toward the big finish.
- Likely to feel like a sharp or well-defined turn in the story, and to occur within one scene.

About A Boy

Break into Act 3: Here, Will tries to go back to his old ways (recommitting to his original story goal), keeping himself busy with shallow pursuits and avoiding any deep or meaningful relationships. Will he succeed, or will he finally realize that "no man is an island"?

Big

Break into Act 3: The list of possible Zoltar locations arrives in the mail at Billy's house. It's what Josh has been waiting for so he can reverse the wish, but Josh is so busy with work and Susan that he ignores Billy's call. It seems as though Josh has become fully entrenched in adulthood, and is content to stay there. The question we're now waiting on the answer to is: will Josh really choose to remain in adulthood, or will he realize the value and fleeting nature of childhood and go back to being thirteen?

Black Swan

Break into Act 3: Nina's solution is to practice even more. During which the pressure and stress bring on a psychotic break, with frightening hallucinations she now cannot escape.

Bridesmaids

Break into Act 3: We see Annie begin to change her ways, saying goodbye to her booty-call Ted. It's the start of her "growth" way of navigating the story. She may have lost everything, but she's also learned a (thematic) lesson and is finally ready to do things differently.

Children of Men

Break into Act 3: The ally who was supposed to help Theo and the young woman get to safety has learned of the baby and now turns on them in an attempt to claim a reward. Theo fights him off and makes a quick getaway with the young woman and her baby. They're on their own again, still trying to reach their destination, now with a baby to protect.

The Conjuring

Break into Act 3: The Perron family takes refuge at a motel, but Carolyn is acting very strange. Meanwhile, the Warrens meet with a priest and learn they'll need Vatican approval for the exorcism. They're told they'll have to wait and hope it comes in time, but we know the problem with Carolyn is going to force their hand – giving us the final showdown of Act 3.

Edge of Tomorrow

Break into Act 3: Cage and Rita make a new plan. They have three hours to kill the alien, and they need to recruit some soldiers who are crazy enough to follow them on this mission. Cage knows just the squad…

Everything Everywhere All At Once

Break into Act 3: Evelyn and Joy meet in another universe as other versions of themselves. Joy confesses that she had secretly hoped that she wouldn't be able to persuade Evelyn over to her nihilistic way of thinking. That perhaps Evelyn would see something she didn't and convince Joy all is not lost, there's another way. This is just enough to begin to turn

Evelyn's thinking, giving her a new direction to pursue as she moves into Act 3.

Ex Machina

Break into Act 3: Caleb tells Ava that she was right about Nathan and his nefarious intentions. Caleb has a plan for them to escape that night.

Ghost

Break into Act 3: Carl sees his money laundering account has been closed, and Sam "haunts" him by making "murderer" appear on the computer screen. This sends Carl back to Molly's to find out what's happening and where his money is... and Sam launches into the final push in pursuit of his story goal: keeping Molly safe.

The Greatest Showman

Break into Act 3: When P.T. learns his assistant, Carlisle, is in the burning building, P.T. runs in looking for him, risking his life to save his friend. P.T. has begun to embrace the thematic lesson, prioritizing the people that matter to him.

Heat

Break into Act 3: Neil calls his connection and asks for three things: Van Zant's address, information on the one-time crew member who has betrayed them, and a new "out" – a way to escape. We know what Neil now wants to accomplish by the end of the movie: revenge on both Van Zant and the traitor, and a clean getaway.

Hidden Figures

Break into Act 3: Collaborating with Al Harrison, Katherine has a math breakthrough that shows how they can get John Glenn home safely. This is the turn in the story that sends us toward the climax.

Hustle

Break into Act 3: The next morning, Stan's daughter gives him an idea to put Boa on social media and piggyback on family friend Dr. J's viral video fame. Stan is reluctant but his wife jumps in to help, making the phone call. This new strategy sends them into Act 3.

The Invisible Man

Break into Act 3: Cecilia attempts suicide to lure out the invisible man and then stabs him, causing his suit to glitch temporarily. The facility's security team arrives but Adrian gets away. But before he does, he threatens to hurt those Cecilia loves, the last two people remaining in her support system. In Act 3, Cecilia must stop the invisible man.

Jumanji: Welcome to the Jungle

Break into Act 3: The players spot their final destination in the distance. Now all they have to do is find a way to get there and replace the jewel. But the villain knows where they are, and he's coming for them.

Little Miss Sunshine

Break into Act 3: Olive unselfishly shows Dwayne she's willing to let go of her own dream in order to support him, and that's enough to get him back in the car. The family gets back on the road for the final push to Olive's beauty pageant.

The Power of the Dog

Break into Act 3: Phil and Peter ride off together to work on a remote part of the ranch. Rose tries to protest, afraid of what might happen, but is unable to stop them. Only one of these men will prevail in the end.

The Proposal

Break into Act 3: Andrew's dad pulls Andrew and Margaret aside and calls their bluff. He's brought the suspicious immigration agent to Sitka and negotiated a deal for Andrew to go unpunished if he flips on Margaret. But Andrew sticks to their story and Margaret follows suit. The wedding is a go.

Ratatouille

Break into Act 3: Adrift, Remy leaves both the restaurant and his rat family behind. He doesn't know where he belongs or where to go next, so at this point his "new plan" is simply to walk away from the things he now believes he's not meant for, or that aren't meant for him.

Shaun of the Dead

Break into Act 3: Shaun discovers that the gun they'd assumed all this time was a prop gun, is real! Shaun now has a new plan to defeat the encroaching zombies, and we move into the final push in this fight for survival.

The Sixth Sense

Break into Act 3: Looking for clues and some way forward, Malcolm goes back to the recordings of his old sessions with Vincent. And... he hears something. Malcolm is finally convinced Cole has been telling the truth, and Malcolm now has an idea about how to help him.

Spider-Man: Into the Spider-Verse

Break into Act 3: After a moving pep talk from his father, Miles is finally able to harness his Spider powers on command. He's ready, determined, and on the move... into Act 3, to complete his mission.

Titanic

Break into Act 3: Rose and Jack finally lose Cal, but they immediately run into flooding in the ship's lower corridors. At least they have each other, and they'll spend Act 3 trying to survive the disaster together.

Top Gun: Maverick

Break into Act 3: Flightboss Cyclone orders, "Send them," and the four jets begin the mission. 'Will they all make it back?' is the question on our minds.

CLIMAX

- The main character's final confrontation with the primary force of opposition.
- Shows us whether the protagonist achieves the story goal or not. It determines the outcome of the story's main conflict.
- Often plays out over a sequence of scenes and feels like a crescendo – which makes sense since it's the culmination of the whole story.

About A Boy

Climax: Will races to the school talent show to save Marcus from embarrassing himself and being ostracized by the other kids. But when he sees that Marcus is willing to do that in order to show Fiona how much he loves her, Will finally understands the thematic lesson this experience is meant to teach him, and does the same for Marcus. Will joins Marcus on stage, ultimately making himself the butt of the joke so that Marcus can get through it unscathed. Rachel is in the audience and sees that Will might truly be a good guy after all. And in the end we see both Will and Marcus with genuine connections, surrounded by friends, family, and love.

Big

Climax: Josh leaves what could be a career-making meeting and goes to find the Zoltar machine, where he makes a new wish to be a kid again. Susan finds him there and Josh must say goodbye to her before returning to his childhood home just as the magic wears off and he's restored to his 13-year-old self.

Black Swan

Climax: Still hallucinating, Nina struggles to perform the opening night of Swan Lake. Between acts, Nina finds Lily in her dressing room. A confrontation turns into a fight and Nina kills her, hiding the body. Nina then takes the stage, dancing flawlessly as the Black Swan. Back in her dressing room she discovers Lily is still alive – and Nina realizes *she's* the one bleeding, having stabbed herself. But Nina goes on to dance the final act of the ballet, which ends with the White Swan throwing herself off a cliff. Nina wows the audience and the other dancers. She has achieved her story goal – to dance the role of Swan Queen. And as she lays dying on stage, Nina tells Thomas, "I felt it. It was perfect," as the screen fades to white.

Bridesmaids

Climax: It's Lillian's wedding day but Annie learns she's nowhere to be found. Annie tracks Lillian down and gives her the pep talk (and dress re-design) Lillian needs in order to walk down the aisle. With this, Annie has repaired her friendship and is back in the wedding party.

Children of Men

Climax: As Theo and the young woman make their way through city streets that have erupted into a war zone, the militant group catches up to them, takes the girl and her baby captive, and orders that Theo be killed. Theo fights his way free, rescues the girl and baby, and manages to get them in sight of the boat to freedom. He dies before he sees them make it, but in his final moments he finally has hope for the future of humanity.

The Conjuring

Climax: Leading up to the climactic scene, the Warrens arrive at the house to find Carolyn trying to kill her daughter April. But when they try to remove Carolyn from the house, her skin begins to burn. Ed will have to perform the exorcism himself, in the house, with the others assisting – this story's final confrontation. During the exorcism, Lorraine helps Carolyn "fight from the inside," by prompting her to recall a happy family memory that Carolyn talked about earlier. Together the group fights off the entity until it's finally gone and Carolyn is free.

Edge of Tomorrow

Climax: Rita and J Squad help Cage fight through an alien attack to reach the aliens' main location. With what looks like his last seconds alive, Cage manages to blow up the source, destroying the alien race's control of the world. When Cage wakes again, the world is different. Humans are victorious, and we know Cage was successful in achieving his story goal.

Everything Everywhere All At Once

Climax: Now fully embracing the thematic lesson, Evelyn finds "something to love" in each universe and uses kindness to battle and disarm each of her opponents: the Alpha jumpers, Deirdre, Gong Gong, Jobu, and finally...

Evelyn and Joy face off in the real world as – despite everything – Joy asks Evelyn to just let her go. Evelyn refuses, telling Joy that no matter what else is possible or the other lives they might have had, and despite any pain involved, Evelyn chooses to be here with Joy and to cherish the few specks of time they have together. When they hug, we know Evelyn has fully accomplished her story goal.

Ex Machina

Climax: Caleb reveals to Nathan that he's modified the security system. They watch as Ava leaves her confinement and confers with Kyoko. Nathan knocks Caleb unconscious and rushes to stop them. He disables Kyoko and damages

Ava in the process, but not before Nathan himself is stabbed. He lays dying while Ava repairs herself and then leaves Caleb locked inside the facility as she escapes on her own into the world.

Ghost

Climax: Carl arrives at Molly's while Sam is in a weakened state. Molly and Oda Mae escape out the window and make it into the vacant loft above. They fight off Carl with Sam's help, and Carl is killed in the process. Molly is now safe; Sam's story goal is achieved. Sam watches as Carl's soul emerges from his body and is taken away by demons. Afterward, we get a nice emotional payoff as well, when Molly is able to see Sam's ghost and he finally tells her he loves her before the angels guide him away.

The Greatest Showman

Climax: P.T. recommits himself to everyone who matters in his life. At the performers' insistence, he vows to find a way to restart the circus. He reunites with his wife, Charity. And he hands off ringmaster duties to Carlisle so P.T. can spend more time watching his daughters grow up. He's finally content with the life he's created.

Heat

Climax: Neil is "home free" but he just can't leave when there's still an opportunity to get revenge on the former crew member who betrayed them. It's a fateful decision as doing so gives Hanna enough time to catch up to Neil, which brings us to the climactic chase scene. It's a cat-and-mouse game on the airport tarmacs, cop vs. robber. Mano a mano. Hanna finally manages to shoot Neil, who dies with Hanna looking on.

Hidden Figures

Climax: On the day of the launch, the IBM's calculations are off. Unless they can be sure of the landing coordinates they'll have to call off the launch and accept defeat. There's only one person John Glenn trusts to confirm the numbers: Katherine. When she's checked all the calculations and the launch is a go, Al Harrison brings her into the control room – recognizing her as a vital part of this mission.

But before they can declare success, there's a tense moment as a warning light alerts the control room that something has gone wrong. Working together, the team provides John Glenn with a manual override solution. Will Katherine's landing coordinates still work? Yes – John Glenn splashes down, safe. Everyone celebrates the accomplishment.

Hustle

Climax: Stan's hard work and relationships prove to pay off as he and Boa get a chance to join a highly exclusive scouting showcase. With Stan's unwavering support, Boa feels the pressure lift and is able to deliver an impressive performance. Stan couldn't be more proud. Then Stan learns he's getting another chance to join the coaching staff, and all of his dreams have come true.

The Invisible Man

Climax: Cecilia agrees to meet Adrian at his house to discuss mending their relationship, but secretly intends to get him to confess so she can record it as proof. When he won't admit all that he's done, she excuses herself. Moments later, the house security camera captures Adrian seemingly slitting his own throat. Cecilia discovers him and calls 911, appearing distraught. But once she's out of the camera's sight, she coolly watches as Adrian lies dying on the floor. When Cecilia leaves, we see she is carrying one of Adrian's "invisibility suits" in her purse, having orchestrated the whole thing.

Jumanji: Welcome to the Jungle

Climax: The villain closes in on the players but they work together and return the jewel to its home in spectacular video game hero fashion. The curse is lifted from Jumanji and the players return to their own world.

Little Miss Sunshine

Climax: Olive takes the stage for her talent performance. Her family watches in the audience, terrified she'll be laughed off the stage. As Olive begins her routine the crowd soon realizes the moves Grandpa taught her are fit for a strip tease. Shocked by the "scandalous" show, the pageant organizer demands Olive be pulled off the stage. Instead, Olive's family joins her on stage to dance with wild abandon, having fun, regardless of what the rest of the world thinks.

The Power of the Dog

Climax: Peter offers Phil some rawhide strips he's cut so that Phil can finish a lasso he's braiding. Phil is moved by this gesture and that night, Phil finishes braiding it as Peter looks on. The next morning, Phil has taken ill. Though he goes to the doctor, he dies quickly – likely from Anthrax. And now we realize the rawhide Peter supplied came from a diseased cow; he deliberately poisoned Phil in order to save Rose from the man's abusive behavior.

The Proposal

Climax: At the altar, Margaret confesses everything and takes responsibility for the ruse. She leaves with the immigration agent, ready to accept her punishment. Andrew goes after her, but is too late. Then, with his family's help, he races to the airport... but is too late again! Back in New York, Margaret is packing up her office when Andrew finally catches up with her and proposes – so they can start dating for real.

Ratatouille

Climax: Remy seizes his dream and proves himself worthy when he commands chefs Linguini and Colette as well as the entire rat colony, to pull off a successful dinner service at the restaurant. Then, Remy finally reveals his true identity to famed food critic Anton Ego, who is convinced of Remy's talent and writes a glowing review –publicly hailing Remy as a chef.

Shaun of the Dead

Climax: Remaining survivors Shaun, Liz, and Ed (who has been bitten but not yet fully turned) make it into the pub cellar where they're momentarily safe, but also trapped – with zombies beating down the door. Shaun laments that he failed everyone, and Liz tells him not to blame himself: "You did something, that's what counts." They quietly debate how to end it, as they only have two shotgun shells left between the three of them. But then Shaun gets one more idea – a possible escape plan. Ed won't go, knowing it's too late for him; he and Shaun must say their goodbyes here. With Ed distracting the zombies, Shaun and Liz make it outside, ready to keep fighting for their lives… just as they see military forces arrive. They didn't give up, and now they're saved!

The Sixth Sense

Climax: Malcolm goes with Cole to help one of the ghosts he's been seeing. It's a young girl who died after being poisoned by her own mother, and now wants to protect her sister from the same fate. This is the first time we've seen Cole unafraid of the ghosts, and able to use his gift to help them instead.

A short time later, Malcolm watches Cole perform in his school play; Cole is now happy and surrounded by friends – Malcolm has finally succeeded at helping him.

Spider-Man: Into the Spider-Verse

Climax: Miles and the rest of the Spider folk defeat Doc Ock and Kingpin's assortment of bad guys, and use the new override key they created to send the Spider folk home to their own dimensions. Then Miles alone faces off with Kingpin. Using his Spider powers and what he learned from his uncle, and buoyed by the love and support of his family, Miles throws Kingpin into the shutoff button. The Collider explodes and the city is saved.

Titanic

Climax: Rose and Jack cling to wreckage in the freezing ocean water. Jack tells her, "Promise me you'll survive." Time passes and finally lifeboats come looking for survivors. Rose comes to and realizes it's too late for Jack – he's already frozen to death. She musters the last of her strength and manages to alert the lifeboats that she is, indeed, alive.

Later, among the survivors, we see Rose avoid Cal. In case there was any question, she's not going back to that old life. At Ellis Island, she gives Jack's last name as her own.

Top Gun: Maverick

Climax: The pilots successfully complete their mission, but now they must get home – a dangerous endeavor in itself, and the part that matters most to Maverick. As they make their way through enemy territory, Rooster finds himself in danger and Maverick intervenes, saving him but getting shot down in the process. On the ground, Maverick is about to be shot but now Rooster intervenes, saving him and getting shot down himself. Which leads us into the final part of this story's climax, as we see Maverick and Rooster work together to get out of enemy territory and back to the aircraft carrier. Once Rooster is safely returned, Maverick's story goal is fully achieved.

A request for your review

Did this book help you in some way? If so, I'd love to hear about it. And reviews help other readers find the right book for their needs too. Please consider leaving a rating or review. I sincerely thank you!

A few final words

While we've reached the end of our movie analysis for now, by this point – after all the theory and examples we've covered – my hope is that you're feeling more confident and excited than ever to continue on your screenwriting journey.

Together, we've studied up on 3-act structure and the Major Plot Points. We've learned how to recognize those important turning points in any movie, and to gauge whether they're functioning effectively. And maybe, if I've done my job well enough, you've even picked up some new ideas about how to strengthen the structure of your own screenplay.

Structure is a tool that good movies use to produce a sense of direction, momentum, and pacing. And in the end, that's all in service to the ultimate goal: creating an effect on the audience. The best thing you can do for your writing is know what effect you're trying to create. Then, use the tools to achieve it in the way that works best for the story you want to tell.

If you'd like to learn more about writing a great screenplay – whether it's your first or your tenth! – you can find additional resources at writeandco.com.

Now – go write that screenplay!

Naomi Beaty

About the author

Naomi Beaty is a screenwriting teacher and consultant who works with writers, producers, and directors at all levels to develop their film and TV projects. Naomi has read thousands of scripts and worked with hundreds of writers, first as a junior development exec at Madonna and Guy Oseary's Maverick Films, and currently through group workshops and one-on-one coaching. She also wrote the bestselling book *The Screenplay Outline Workbook: A step-by-step guide to brainstorm ideas, structure your story, and prepare to write your best screenplay.*

Credits for movies referenced in this book

BIG (1988)

> Written by Gary Ross & Anne Spielberg
>
> Directed by Penny Marshall

GHOST (1990)

> Written by Bruce Joel Rubin
>
> Directed by Jerry Zucker

HEAT (1995)

> Written and directed by Michael Mann

TITANIC (1997)

> Written and directed by James Cameron

THE SIXTH SENSE (1999)

> Written and directed by M. Night Shyamalan

ABOUT A BOY (2002)

> Screenplay by Peter Hedges and Chris Weitz & Paul Weitz, based on the novel by Nick Hornby
>
> Directed by Chris Weitz & Paul Weitz

SHAUN OF THE DEAD (2004)

Written by Simon Pegg and Edgar Wright

Directed by Edgar Wright

CHILDREN OF MEN (2006)

Screenplay by Alfonso Cuaron & Timothy J. Sexton and David Arata and Mark Fergus & Hawk Ostby, based on the novel by P.D. James

Directed by Alfonso Cuaron

LITTLE MISS SUNSHINE (2006)

Written by Michael Arndt

Directed by Jonathan Dayton and Valerie Faris

RATATOUILLE (2007)

Written by Brad Bird

Original story by Jan Pinkava & Jim Capobianco & Brad Bird

Additional story material by Emily Cook & Kathy Greenberg and Bob Peterson

Directed by Brad Bird, Co-director Jan Pinkava

THE PROPOSAL (2009)

Written by Peter Chiarelli

Directed by Anne Fletcher

BLACK SWAN (2010)

Screenplay by Mark Heyman and Andres Heinz and John J. McLaughlin

Story by Andres Heinz

Directed by Darren Aronofsky

BRIDESMAIDS (2011)

Written by Kristen Wiig & Annie Mumolo

Directed by Paul Feig

THE CONJURING (2013)

Written by Chad Hayes & Carey W. Hayes

Directed by James Wan

EDGE OF TOMORROW (2014)

Screenplay by Christopher McQuarrie and Jez Butterworth & John-Henry Butterworth, based on a novel by Hiroshi Sakurazaka

Directed by Doug Liman

EX MACHINA (2014)

Written and directed by Alex Garland

HIDDEN FIGURES (2016)

Screenplay by Allison Schroeder and Theodore Melfi, based on the book by Margot Lee Shetterly

Directed by Theodore Melfi

THE GREATEST SHOWMAN (2017)

Screenplay by Jenny Bicks and Bill Condon

Story by Jenny Bicks

Directed by Michael Gracey

JUMANJI: WELCOME TO THE JUNGLE (2017)

Screenplay by Chris McKenna & Erik Sommers and Scott Rosenberg & Jeff Pinkner

Screen story by Chris McKenna

Based on the film "Jumanji" screenplay by Jonathan Hensleigh and Greg Taylor & Jim Strain

Based on the film "Jumanji" screen story by Greg Taylor and Chris Van Allsburg

Based on the film "Jumanji" by Jim Strain

Based on the book by Chris Van Allsburg

Directed by Jake Kasdan

SPIDER-MAN: INTO THE SPIDER-VERSE (2018)

Screenplay by Phil Lord and Rodney Rothman

Story by Phil Lord

Directed by Bob Persichetti, Peter Ramsey, and Rodney Rothman

THE INVISIBLE MAN (2020)

Screenplay by Leigh Whannell

Screen story by Leigh Whannell

Directed by Leigh Whannell

THE POWER OF THE DOG (2021)

Written and directed by Jane Campion

Based on the novel by Thomas Savage

EVERYTHING EVERYWHERE ALL AT ONCE (2022)

Written by Daniel Kwan & Daniel Scheinert

Directed by Daniel Kwan and Daniel Scheinert

HUSTLE (2022)

Written by Taylor Materne and Will Fetters

Directed by Jeremiah Zagar

TOP GUN: MAVERICK (2022)

Screenplay by Ehren Kruger and Eric Warren Singer and Christopher McQuarrie

Story by Peter Craig and Justin Marks

Based on characters created by Jim Cash & Jack Epps Jr.

Directed by Joseph Kosinski

Printed in Great Britain
by Amazon

39627015R00089